Wx 400 THO   SATH

Loss, Grief and Trauma in the Workplace

Neil Thompson
Liverpool Hope University, United Kingdom

Death, Value, and Meaning Series
Series Editor: Dale A. Lund

Baywood Publishing Company, Inc.
AMITYVILLE, NEW YORK

Baywood Publishing Company, Inc.
26 Austin Avenue
P.O. Box 337
Amityville, NY 11701
(800) 638-7819
E-mail: baywood@baywood.com
Web site: baywood.com

Library of Congress Catalog Number: 2008034867
ISBN: 978-0-89503-342-0 (cloth)

Library of Congress Cataloging-in-Publication Data

Thompson, Neil, 1955-
    Loss, grief, and trauma in the workplace / by Neil Thompson.
        p. cm. -- (Death, value, and meaning series)
    Includes bibliographical references (p.   ) and index.
    ISBN 978-0-89503-342-0 (cloth : alk. paper) 1. Psychology, Industrial. 2. Interpersonal relations. 3. Employees--Psychological aspects. 4. Management--Psychological aspects. 5. Quality of work life. I. Title.
    HF5548.8.T487 2008
    158.7--dc22

                                                2008034867

Dedication

For Sid and Miriam

Table of Contents

Foreword

Neil Thompson's *Loss, Grief and Trauma in the Workplace* is a seminal and groundbreaking work. Work is what people do. People also experience loss, grief and trauma. Few of us are prepared for crises when they occur. With this wise and accessible book on loss, grief and trauma in the workplace, Neil Thompson has added an extraordinary achievement to an already distinguished career. With Neil's framework and case examples, the reader is guided with a roadmap of helping approaches and an entire conceptual array of tools that will allow all of us in our workplaces to better manage when loss, grief and trauma occur.

This book's value will be measured by those who use it to manage loss, grief and trauma in the workplace. It is written in a style that allows both the professional and the non-professional to gain insights and strategies to manage crises in the workplace. Professionals in the field will find that Neil has included the latest concepts, theories, research, models, and practice in this accessible volume. At the same time, he is able to write in a style that allows those in the workplace who are not professionals to gain immense insights into social attitudes and values, a clearer understanding of relationships, a better appreciation of the multiple layers of fateful circumstances that are a part of all of our lives, and means of coping within the workplace. Unlike many books in the field, it is not based upon a clinical population. Neil uses workplace situations and offers a solid theoretical analysis of how to cope. A manager, worker, or family member of a worker can gain from reading this book as well as the seasoned professional.

The book has seven chapters. The author attempts to blend theory and practice into each of them. Chapter 1 presents the major concepts and theories relating to loss, grief and trauma. In this short chapter, he is able to summarize the material presented in entire books. He ends with an analysis of the implications of terrorism using practice examples. Chapter 2 examines loss in the workplace, including both theoretical and practical examples of the impact of loss in the workplace, re-learning the world, meaning making, ritual, and corporate responsibility. Neil ends the chapter with an examination of workplace well-being and its impact on the organization. Chapter 3 is also a theoretical chapter that analyzes trauma in the workplace. This chapter would also have value for educators as it includes bullying, harassment, aggression, abuse, and violence among other concepts. He also includes suggestions for dealing with trauma in the workplace. The first three chapters cover the major theories and developments in the field and apply them to practice. Chapter 4 examines policy. Mine disasters, construction accidents, terroristic acts, or other traumatic workplace events require working with families, media liaison, commemoration rituals, and legal issues. This chapter offers suggestions for managing such issues. Chapter 5 provides suggestions for providing care and support of staff and creating workplace well-being. Chapter 6 offers dos and don'ts of helping in the workplace. It is an excellent chapter. Chapter 7 puts together all of the ideas, policies, practices, theories, and concepts and suggests ways to gain further knowledge and learning.

While there are many books on terrorism and trauma, few discuss how to manage terrorism and trauma in the workplace. Neil offers images of growth rather than psychopathology as the best way to manage trauma of terrorism. His work represents one of the few in the field that combines the best of practice and research through a lens that is not clouded by a psychiatric view. While there are clearly people who may need professional help to cope, most of us are expected to continue to work, produce, and to "move on" when loss, grief and trauma occur. Loss, grief and trauma touch all of our lives. The reality of death is a part of all of our lives. Rather than simply offering a clinical solution, Neil provides clear, practical suggestions for aiding those who are grieving or traumatized. He suggests that simply "being there" and showing care and concern can be an important source of support. Rather than avoiding the painful situations that accompany loss, grief and trauma, Neil suggests that we need to connect with the person and not trivialize them or their situation. This practical, yet strongly theoretical volume has been missing for far too long. It is a great contribution to the field and to those in the workplace who experience loss, grief and trauma and to those who are with them in the workplace.

Neil is able to offer the reader a solid, practical, theoretical analysis of loss, grief and trauma in the workplace. He offers pathways to understanding, improving, and learning from painful life experiences. He recognizes that all workplace environments are not the same nor are all losses and traumas, but he does provide a pathway to manage losses and trauma in the workplace that I have not found in any other book. I would recommend this book for professionals in the bereavement field, for teachers, for corporate executives, parents, workers, students, families, and anyone who is working or has worked. All of us must deal with loss, grief bullying, trauma, crises, and dramatic events. Neil is a fierce advocate. I would want him to be on my team when loss, grief or trauma occurs in the workplace. Neil offers a solid, competent, research-based, yet practical book on workplace loss. This small volume will change the field and also allow many of us to better manage loss, grief and trauma in the workplace. I thank him for writing such an excellent book.

Dr. Gerry R. Cox
Director, Center for Death Education and Bioethics
University of Wisconsin–La Crosse

Preface

Work is an important part of most people's lives—for example, in terms of how it plays a part in shaping our identity and our network of social relationships. Therefore, given how much time most of us spend in the workplace, it would be very unwise not to give careful consideration to how workplace issues influence us and make a major contribution (positively or negatively) to our well-being. The world of work is therefore one that can be very meaningful for us and can play a significant role in determining how satisfied we are with our lives, how fulfilling or otherwise our experiences are and how 'at one' we feel with our world. In other words, the workplace is part of our spirituality [1].

Where problems arise in the workplace, they can therefore have very significant and far-reaching consequences. As a general rule, then, workplace problems can be seen to merit close attention, even though so much of the management and human resources literature fails to address such issues. This book is intended to rectify that imbalance in part by addressing one set of workplace problems—namely those that arise from experiences of loss, grief and trauma. Such problems can arise within the workplace itself or can be 'imported' into the work setting from employees' personal lives. Either way, their impact on the individuals concerned and the wider work community can be immense.

This book should therefore be of interest and value to anyone concerned with workplace matters and/or loss, grief and trauma as social and psychological phenomena. This will include:

- Managers and human resources professionals who are keen to develop their understanding of how the very real problems of loss, grief and trauma can best be tackled where and when they arise in work settings and, where possible, prevented from occurring in the first place. This will include practicing managers and human resources professionals who want to learn about the challenges they may be facing now or at any time in the future as well as those pursuing educational programs that should prepare them for a career in people management (an MBA, for example).

- People involved in tackling human problems in the workplace in general and those relating to loss, grief and trauma in particular. This will include occupational health professionals (including psychiatrists), counselors, social workers, psychologists, the clergy, and people employed in employee assistance programs (EAPs). Again, this will apply to those already practicing in these areas and who wish to deepen their understanding and extend their knowledge base, as well as those pursuing educational programs geared towards becoming professionally qualified in one of the disciplines mentioned.
- Scholars and students in a broad range of academic disciplines that incorporate either workplace issues, loss, grief and trauma concerns or both. This would include sociology, psychology, industrial relations and applied social studies.

And, of course, this list of potential readers of this book does not exclude the interested general reader curious to find out more about the fascinating issues that arise when two worlds not normally connected in the popular consciousness come together—the everyday world of work and the very challenging world of loss, grief and trauma.

In writing the book I have been very careful to blend theory and practice. In this way, the book can be used as a means of building up knowledge and understanding of the complexities involved purely as an educational exercise in its own right, or it can be used as a source book to inform efforts to address at a practical level the problems and challenges identified. That is, it can be used as a general contribution to developing our understanding of this largely under-researched area of social life and thus be a platform for further learning and practice, or it can be used in a more focused, specific way to help inform efforts to help—for example, some of the guidelines presented could form the basis of discussions within an organization about how to tackle a particular situation that has arisen. Either way, it is to be hoped that what is offered within these pages will be of value in helping not only to raise awareness of the importance of the subject matter, but also to develop our understanding of the subtleties involved in a very complex aspect of organizational life.

REFERENCE

1. B. Moss, *Religion and Spirituality,* Russell House Publishing, Lyme Regis, United Kingdom, 2005.

Acknowledgments

There are many people I owe a vote of thanks for their support in completing this book. Dr. Dale Lund, as series editor, has been very helpful and I am grateful to him for the faith he has shown in my work. I am also considerably indebted to Dr. Gerry Cox of the University of Wisconsin–La Crosse for his very supportive Foreword.

I am very grateful to Dr. Dick Gilbert, of the World Pastoral Care Center/Bridge Builders; Dr. Howard Stein of the University of Oklahoma; and Dr. Louise Rowling of the University of Sydney for their endorsement of the book and their helpful comments on it.

In terms of moral and practical support, Susan Thompson, Anna Thompson and Dr. Sharon Brimfield-Edwards, all of Avenue Consulting Ltd., have proven invaluable. I very much appreciate their backing.

It is also important that I express my gratitude for the comments and advice received from Bernard Moss of Staffordshire University, England; Graham Thompson of Bangor University, Wales; Jon Mills of Hope House Hospice, England; and my Australian friends Mary Tehan and Irene Renzenbrink.

Last but not least, I wish to thank Sid and Miriam Moss, well-known authors and well-respected researchers in the loss and grief field, for their support and friendship over the years. I have learned so much from them. It is for these reasons that the book is dedicated to them.

About the Author

Neil Thompson, PhD is a Director of Avenue Consulting LTD (www.avenue consulting.co.uk), a company based in Wales offering training and consultancy services in relation to social and occupational well-being. He has held four full or honorary professorships at UK universities and has over 100 publications to his name, including best-selling textbooks, papers in learned journals and training and open learning materials. His recent books include:

> *People Skills* (Palgrave Macmillan, 2nd edn, 2002)
> *Promoting Equality* (Palgrave Macmillan, 2nd edn, 2003)
> *Communication and Language: A Handbook of Theory and Practice* (Palgrave Macmillan, 2003)
> *People Problems* (Palgrave Macmillan, 2006)
> *Promoting Workplace Learning* (Policy Press, 2006)
> *Power and Empowerment* (Russell House Publishing, 2007)
> *The Critically Reflective Practitioner* (with Sue Thompson, Palgrave Macmillan, 2008)

He also edited the book *Loss and Grief: A Guide for Human Services Practitioners* (Palgrave Macmillan, 2002) that contains contributions from leading international thinkers in the field, including a Foreword by the late Dr. John D. Morgan.

Neil has over 30 years experience as a practitioner, manager, educator, consultant and expert witness in the human services. He is very well respected for his ability to communicate complex ideas in an accessible way without oversimplifying them.

He has been a speaker at seminars and conferences in the UK, Ireland, Greece, the Netherlands, Norway, the Czech Republic, Spain, Italy, Hong Kong, India, Canada, the United States and Australia and has qualifications in social work, management (MBA), training and development, mediation and dispute resolution, as well as a first-class honors degree in Social Sciences and a PhD.

Neil is a Chartered Fellow of the Chartered Institute of Personnel and Development in the UK and a Fellow of the Royal Society of Arts (elected to the latter on the basis of his contribution to workplace learning). He is also a Fellow of the Higher Education Academy and a Life Fellow of the Institute of Welsh Affairs. In addition, he is a member of the International Work Group on Death, Dying and Bereavement.

Neil has recently become the editor of the international journal, *Illness, Crisis & Loss* (published by Baywood). He was previously the guest editor of a special issue of the journal on the subject of "Loss and Grief in the Workplace." He also currently edits the free quarterly e-zine, *Well-being* (www.well-being.org.uk). He is a sought-after conference speaker, consultant, and workshop facilitator. His personal Website is at www.neilthompson.info.

Introduction

The German philosopher, Martin Heidegger, writing early in the last century, described human existence as *being-towards-death* [1].What he meant by this is that we are finite creatures; each of us is steadily moving towards death. Even though many people may live their lives as though they regard themselves as immortal, they are of course deluding themselves. To deny the reality of death is not only absurdly illogical, it also means that we are likely to be ill-equipped when we are touched by death in some way (the loss of a loved one, for example) and, of perhaps equal importance, we are less likely to gain the maximum benefits that can accrue from valuing each day as a precious and limited resource, to appreciate our time on this earth and not waste it. In other words, it is not only wisely realistic to take account of the fact that we have a finite lifespan and will all one day die, it is also enriching—it can help us develop more spiritually fulfilling and meaningful lives.

These comments apply to life in general, but my particular concern in this book is how these matters are reflected in the workplace. This is because the general tendency to ignore the finite nature of human existence can be seen to be especially evident in organizational life. Where the main concern is "the bottom line" or achieving other corporate objectives, it is very easy for key issues about being human to slip to the bottom of the priority list—or even off the agenda altogether. And, of course, a workplace that neglects the human dimension risks being not only an oppressive and destructive place for its employees, but also an unsuccessful and ineffective organization as a consequence of mistreating its most important resource—its people.

VALUING PEOPLE

The need to take seriously the "people factor" in organizational life has received increasing attention in recent years. In fact, the idea that an organization's most important resource is its human resource has become very well established as a management principle. While I regard it as a positive development that such concerns are being taken very seriously, I must admit to having some anxiety about the fact that, in some quarters at least, it has become a slogan—perhaps an empty slogan, the implications of which have not been carefully thought through.

One approach to human resources that does justice to the implications of the need to value people ("the human resource") is the emerging field of "workplace well-being." The Canadian Office of Public Service Values and Ethics offers helpful comment when they define workplace well-being as:

> a holistic approach to creating high performance organizations through establishing the right conditions to generate high levels of employee engagement. Workplace Well-being is connected to physical health, mental health and wellness but primarily emphasizes the social and psychological dimensions of three inter-related elements—workplace, workforce, and the work people do. [2]

The need to address loss, grief and trauma in the workplace can be seen as part of workplace well-being, insofar as the concerns associated with these issues can stand in the way of organizational effectiveness if they are not addressed properly. This book, then, helps to set loss, grief and trauma in the context of the value of developing a workplace well-being approach.

Unfortunately, while workplace well-being issues are receiving increasing attention, the need for such well-being is also increasing, insofar as there is evidence to suggest that many organizations are valuing their employees less, rather than more. Ehrenreich refers to the work of management consultant David Noer, who observes that:

> Organizations that used to see people as long-term assets to be nurtured and developed now see people as short-term costs to be reduced . . . [T]hey view people as "things" that are but one variable in the production equation, "things" that can be discarded when the profit and loss numbers do not come out as desired. [3, p. 225]

Such developments, that are also identified by Allcorn [4], Stein [5], and Uchitelle [6], make it even more imperative that we take seriously the challenge of promoting workplace well-being.

LOSS: BREADTH AND DEPTH

While the need to take account of how death-related issues impact on the workplace is clearly important, we should not fail to recognize that there is an extensive range of significant losses that are not connected with death. These include divorce or other relationship breakdown; becoming disabled or chronically sick; being a victim of crime (and thus losing confidence and/or a sense of security), layoffs; and many others. This book is therefore not only about death-related losses, but also about the other widespread and often very significant losses that are part and parcel of life in general and working life in particular.

But it is not only the breadth of loss factors that is worthy of our attention. There is also the matter of the *depth* of loss, the profound differences (positive or negative) that the experience of loss can make to individuals, groups and organizations. A loss experience can have life-changing consequences; it can be a 'critical moment' that amounts to a point of no return. We should not therefore make the mistake of assuming that dealing with loss issues is simply a matter of making comforting noises and offering solace to grieving individuals. As we shall see, the reality is far more complex and profound than this.

Being equipped to tackle these complexities is quite a challenging enterprise. This book will not provide all the answers, but it will provide a sound foundation on which to build a better understanding—and thus a platform for developing workable strategies that suit the culture and needs of the organization concerned.

TRAUMA AND THE TERRORIST THREAT

Psychological trauma can apply to any individual at any time—no one is immune. In the workplace, then, it is only a matter of time before trauma plays a part. However, we also need to recognize that trauma can happen to a group of people—for example, as a result of a disaster. Such disasters can arise as a result of natural events (such as floods or hurricanes), technological failure (plane crashes) or deliberate individual actions (a mass shooting). However, we also have to contend with another category of disaster that has received increasing interest in recent years—that is, disasters associated with terrorism. This clearly applies when an actual attack takes place, but can also arise in circumstances where there is no actual attack, but the threat of one is sufficient to cause problems—for example, people being crushed to death in a stampede as a result of a panic arising from a false alarm. It is therefore sadly the case that even an assumed threat of terrorism that has no actual basis in reality can have the effect of bringing about a traumatic reaction for a large number of people.

In these days of heightened awareness of potential acts of terrorism, the need to understand, and be ready to deal with, trauma in the workplace is particularly acute. Organizations that simply hope it will never happen and thus take no preparatory steps for mounting a response may well be lucky enough to get away with it. However, it is an enormous set of risks to take. A much wiser approach is to take the trouble of learning more about trauma and its implications and trying to be as reasonably prepared as we can.

A HISTORY OF NEGLECT

Loss, grief and trauma are subjects that have tended to be neglected in the management and human resources literature and, equally, the workplace has been a neglected area of thanatological study (that is, the study of death and related matters) and indeed the study of loss and grief more broadly. It is therefore fair to say that the subject matter of this book has been doubly neglected to date. This is a very worrying and unsatisfactory state of affairs for, as we shall see as the book unfolds, the challenges involved are of significant proportions and the costs of not taking these challenges seriously can be immense. This book is therefore an important counterbalance to this history of relative neglect, and it is to be hoped that it can play an important role in stimulating further study, debate, reflection, research and policy development.

PLAN OF THE BOOK

The book is divided into seven chapters, each of which seeks to blend theory and practice. The first three chapters have more of a focus on theory, while Chapters 4 to 6 place greater emphasis on practice.

Chapter 1 lays down the foundations by providing an overview of some of the key points about loss, grief and trauma that we will need to understand if we are to put ourselves in a sufficiently strong position to be able to respond to the problems that arise and, ideally, to be able to prevent them where possible.

Chapter 2 builds on this by examining how significant loss and grief issues are in the workplace and how dangerous it is not to prepare ourselves for dealing with them. Chapter 3 plays a similar role by focusing on how trauma can have profound and far-reaching consequences for organizations—particularly for those who have not taken any preparatory steps to minimize the negative impact that can reach major proportions in some situations.

Chapter 4 explores some of the key legal and policy requirements that apply to loss, grief and trauma as they apply to work settings. It does not provide a comprehensive legal and policy guide, but it does provide a firm basis for organizations to meet their legal duties (for example, in relation to health and safety) and to develop policies that are likely to be effective and helpful.

Chapter 5 has the title of *Providing Care and Support*. It is concerned with identifying the support needs of staff and managers working within or on behalf of organizations that are dealing with grief and trauma reactions. Grief and trauma are not, of course, contagious diseases, but the psychological and social processes involved can conspire to produce a situation that is stressful and harmful for those who are trying to provide help and care. The need to focus on supporting caregivers is another important aspect of this subject matter.

Chapter 6 is entitled *Helps and Hindrances*. It comprises a set of guidelines on what can be helpful in dealing with these very complex and sensitive matters, together with a discussion of the pitfalls to be avoided—the mistakes and mis-understandings that can fail to produce positive progress and may actually make matters worse.

Chapter 7 is the conclusion and serves the purpose of summarizing the key themes developed throughout the book and sets the scene for further learning and development. This emphasis on further learning is reinforced in the *Guide to Further Learning* which contains information and guidance on further reading, in journals, training materials, organizations and websites.

The book covers some vitally important issues that have a history of being neglected despite the potentially disastrous consequences of failing to be prepared for them. It will not provide you with everything you need to know on the subject, but it should provide a sound foundation and an impetus for you to develop your knowledge and understanding further. It should also help you and motivate you to become engaged in the very real challenges of making the workplace an environment that is positive, nurturing and supportive at times of extreme need and vulnerability—an engagement that can be of immense benefit to all concerned.

Some people may find the subject matter difficult or worrying, as it involves facing up to some very challenging issues. It is to be hoped, though, that the understanding and guidance the book offers will help readers to feel better equipped to deal with these challenges. The book should also make it clear why it is essential that we do face up to these issues, as a strategy of pretending they do not apply to us or to our workplace is a dangerously misguided one. Perhaps the wisdom of the east can help us in this regard, particularly Krishnamurti's comment to the effect that: "Facts are not frightening. But if you try to avoid them, turn your back and run, then that is frightening" [7].

REFERENCES

1. M. Heidegger, *Being and Time*, Blackwell, Oxford, 1962 (German original published 1927).
2. Canadian Office of Public Service Values and Ethics (http://www.hrma-agrh.gc.ca/hr-rh/wlbps-eeoppfps/index_e.asp)
3. B. Ehrenreich, *Bait and Switch: The (Futile) Pursuit of the American Dream*, Metropolitan Books, New York, 2005.
4. S. Allcorn, *Death of the Spirit in the American Workplace*, Quorum Books, Westport, Connecticut, 2001.
5. H. F. Stein, *Insight and Imagination: A Study in Knowing and Not-Knowing in Organizational Life*, University Press of America, Lanham, Maryland, 2007.
6. L. Uchitelle, *The Disposable American: Layoffs and Their Consequences*, Vintage Books, New York, 2007.
7. M. Luytens (ed.), *Freedom from the Known*, Krishnamurti Foundation Trust, 1969.

CHAPTER 1
Understanding Loss, Grief and Trauma

Death and dying, and loss more broadly, are subjects that many people do not want to face up to and will therefore try to avoid where possible. While this is perfectly understandable up to a point, it can be very unhelpful. It can prevent us from developing an understanding of how significant such matters are in the workplace and can leave us ill-prepared to deal with the not in considerable challenges they can present.

It is important to recognize that loss and grief are basic parts of human existence for all of us all of the time and, for many people at various points in their life, trauma is also a fundamental occurrence that can have significant implications. In trying to understand issues relating to loss, grief and trauma it is essential to realize that they can be extremely complex but, unfortunately, are often oversimplified and misunderstood. There is some evidence to suggest that we are moving away from this tendency now (as a result of the growing influence of the death education movement, for example), but it would be overoptimistic to think that we have left the problems behind us entirely.

What adds to this difficulty is the fact that the issues are often swept under the carpet as a result of our strong tendency, in western cultures at least, to have a denial of mortality. As DeSpelder and Strickland put it: "Death may be devalued, even denied for a time, but it cannot be eluded" [1, p. 529]. Many modern societies nonetheless operate as if death and loss are not inevitable for us. This can leave so many people very unprepared when a significant loss does arise. It also means that people often do not appreciate what they have and constantly strive for more (in terms of consumerism, for example) because, by denying the finite nature of human existence in this way, the value of what we have can be missed. This can be seen as an important part of both spirituality and well-being—trying to find meaning and fulfilment beyond such superficial matters as consumer goods or other such mundane considerations. As Feifel [2] has argued, appreciating the finite nature of human existence can bring enriched levels of self-knowledge and promote creativity.

As noted in the Introduction, loss, grief and trauma are very important in the workplace, even if they are not recognized as such. However, before addressing these issues in a workplace context, it is important to lay the foundations of understanding. This will involve exploring the key issues relating to each of the three—that is, loss, grief and trauma:

- *Loss.* What part does loss play in everyday life? How does it feature in shaping important aspects of our lives?
- *Grief.* How does the experience of grief make a difference in people's lives? How can we deal with the challenges it presents?
- *Trauma.* How can certain life experiences "wound" us? How can we best respond to such circumstances?

I shall therefore explore in turn each of these three areas. I shall provide a basic introduction to some of the key issues relating first to loss, then to grief and finally to trauma. However, it has to be noted that, in the space available, these can be only basic introductions, and readers wishing to develop their understanding further are advised to consult the *Guide to Further Learning* at the end of the book where you will find signposts to opportunities to develop your understanding further by reference to additional reading material, and details of organizations and websites.

LOSS

It would be a significant mistake not to recognize that loss is a basic part of life. Every time we gain something, we lose something else. For example, in gaining sophistication, we lose innocence. As one door opens, other doors close. This is not necessarily a problem, but simply a recognition of how significant loss is as a fundamental part of human existence. How significant a particular loss is to us will depend on how much we have invested in what is lost. This introduces the Freudian notion of "cathexis," a term used to refer to the emotional investment we make in a person, a thing, a relationship, or whatever. When we lose that person, thing or relationship, we then lose the emotions we had invested. It is the equivalent of a Wall Street crash and can be very painful and disconcerting for all concerned, with significant wide-ranging implications.

Practice Focus 1.1

Lyn was devastated when she discovered that her sister, Kate, had been killed in a road traffic accident. Kate, the elder of the two, had been a role model for Lyn, especially in her adolescent years in which she had encountered quite a few problems. As Kate had also become a mother first, she was a great help when Lyn gave birth.

Even though Lyn's reaction to the news of her sister's death was one of shock and disbelief, it was not long before she became aware of how much she had lost, of how big a gap in her life the loss of Kate would leave. She felt so empty inside, so desperately sad and bereft. She wondered if her life would ever be the same again. So much positive emotion had gone into her relationship with Kate and now she felt as though it had just disappeared, vanished into thin air. It was the worst feeling she had ever known in her life.

The Range of Losses

Loss is often equated with bereavement—that is, with death-related losses—but, again the reality is much more complex than this. Loss can occur in a variety of ways, chiefly the following:

- *Power or status.* When we encounter layoffs, redeployment or restructuring, we can experience a loss of power or status, and that can be quite significant in terms of how we experience our lives in general and that proportion of our time we spend in the workplace in particular.
- *Ability.* The onset of disability, ill-health or possibly other changes of circumstances, can lead to a loss of ability. For example, technological change can mean that somebody's ability in a particular area is no longer required, because the technology to which it relates is no longer used.
- *Hope, ambition or aspiration.* All of these can be lost when we miss a certain opportunity or again when circumstances change. Disappointment is, in effect, a form of grief reaction to a loss. Examples would include a project being cancelled after a lot of time, effort and energy have been invested in it, and applying for a job but being unsuccessful.
- *Relationship or connection.* Where we fall out with a friend or colleague or he or she moves away or changes job, we can again experience a significant loss. This can sometimes be as a result of conflict occurring, but is often due to changes in circumstances beyond our control—for example, a job relocation to a new area imposed on an employee.
- *Meaning.* This can occur in two ways. First, we can lose a specific meaning—for example, when someone has a crisis of faith—or second, we can also experience a loss of meaning as a result of other losses. For example, someone who is made redundant may, for a certain time at least, lose their sense of career—that is, what their working life means to them and how it might develop. As Lattanzi-Licht puts it:

> Many people who endure a profound loss experience a crisis of meaning. Things that seemed important or worth working toward are now thrown into question. Part of the personal searching that follows a major loss centers on a re-ordering of values and priorities. In that re-evaluation, one's work may, at least in the short run, become less significant. [3, pp. 21–22]

This is a point which we shall return below.

- *Security.* We each have particular ways of feeling secure. We develop points of reference or "landmarks" that help give a sense of familiarity, comfort and safety. When one of these landmarks of security is lost, we can begin to feel very insecure. Loss of security can be particularly problematic when it is either *multiple* (that is, several landmarks of security are lost at the same time) or *cumulative* (that is, when one loss of security is followed by another and another, and so on).
- *Respect and honor.* When we experience a situation characterized by guilt or shame, we can lose respect and honor. This can happen in one of two ways. It can arise where such a loss of respect and honor is justified (that is, where we have indeed acted shamefully) or equally, it can occur in circumstances where it is not justified, when we have not behaved in an unacceptable manner, but circumstances conspire to give people the impression that we have. Whether the loss of honor and respect is justified or not, its impact can be just as potent. Loss of respect can also include loss of self-respect and thus of confidence which, in turn, can lead to other losses, such as capability in certain areas or even of employment.

This is not a comprehensive list, but merely a reflection of some of the main ways in which loss can affect us, irrespective of whether or not someone close to us has died. However, what we also have to recognize is that many of these losses additionally arise when a death does occur, and so there is not always a clear dividing line between a death-related loss and one that is not death related. The two can overlap and interweave quite considerably. Indeed, this is a characteristic of losses in general—that they are interconnected—and so one loss can trigger or exacerbate others. For example, as noted above, loss of status may result in a loss of confidence. That, in turn, may lead to a loss of security, and that loss of security may undermine a relationship, perhaps leading, after a time, to the loss of that relationship. This pattern may even lead to the development of a vicious circle in which a series of losses reinforce one another in ways that lead to an acceleration over time. Clearly, this can be quite a harmful situation when it develops, and is therefore one that we should seek to avoid.

Rituals

Another important point that we need to bear in mind is that death-related losses often have rituals associated with them that have the effect of bringing people together and generating support and a sense of "this is difficult, but at least we are in it together." Rituals, in effect, are acts imbued with meaning [4], and that also makes them very significant. However, losses that are not death related often have no equivalent rituals (although some may—for example, the leaving "do" or retirement party and gold watch). The absence of rituals can make losses more difficult to deal with.

Without social rituals, a loss can become associated with isolation, rather than solidarity, and there may even be a sense of shame associated with a loss (see the discussion of disenfranchised grief below). This is because one of the common reactions to a loss is a sense of guilt, a sense of "if only. . . ." It is very easy for this feeling to become converted to an irrational sense of shame. Rituals can be very useful for making it clear that the loss is not a matter of shame but, in the absence of rituals, the grieving persons can face additional problems—the impact can be compounded. Irion captures the point well when he argues that:

> By understanding the ways in which rituals can help mourners to cope with their grief, individuals and families can benefit by participating in traditional rituals or in devising new ritual responses to their loss. Effective use of such rituals makes movement from the former reality to the new reality not only possible but empowering. [5, p. 165]

Rituals can also be significant parts of faith communities. Being a member of a particular religion or faith group will generally involve access to certain ritual practices. When it comes to loss-related rituals, however, it is likely to be the case that death-related losses will be better served than other forms of loss.

From these brief comments, it should be more than apparent that loss is therefore much more common than most people may generally realize, and that also it is much more significant as a factor in people's lives—including their working lives. This is an important theme that will be developed throughout the book.

GRIEF

Grief can be seen as our psychological reaction to loss. It is generally characterized by a sense of emptiness or absence. Although grief is a phenomenon that can—and will—apply to every human being, it is important to be aware that grieving is not a case of "one size fits all." For many years, grief was presented as primarily a biological process, and therefore assumed to be pretty much the same for everybody. However, theoretical developments and research evidence have combined to convince us that this is not a helpful way of seeing grief. We now recognize that different people grieve differently, and there will be significant differences between individuals and across groups.

Common Patterns in Grief

Nonetheless, despite these significant differences, there are also common patterns to our grief reactions. That is, underpinning the differences involved will be recurring themes; they will not apply to all grieving people at all times, but will reflect common patterns. These common themes can be characterized in terms of four different types:

- *Physical.* There can be significant physical reactions to a loss. These include loss of appetite or even its opposite, comfort eating; headaches;

stomach aches; debility—basically, the physical reactions associated with stress. As with stress, there can also be an exacerbation of existing health problems—asthma, for example.

- *Emotional.* Anger, guilt, sadness, depression, irritability—these can all be experienced as a result of a grief reaction. Emotions are not simply individualized, psychological reactions—they are also social and interpersonal phenomena. The emotional dimension of grief therefore has to be understood in broad terms and not simply as a personal or individual matter.

- *Cognitive.* This can include difficulty in concentrating or thinking clearly and memory impairment. Such problems can fluctuate and may be influenced by other factors, such as tiredness or having a headache.

- *Behavioral.* This can include withdrawal, impatience, aggression or a lack of competence in using machinery (this final point being linked in many cases to the cognitive problems outlined above). In many cases, grief-related behaviors may be misinterpreted as evidence of something else; for example, withdrawal may be misconstrued as a lack of commitment or as laziness.

Although these four dimensions have been presented separately, we have to be aware that, in reality, they interact and reinforce each other. What is also important to acknowledge is that grief is often referred to as our *emotional* response to a loss but, as these comments indicate, it is more than emotional, it is psychological in the broader sense and does not limit itself to the feelings dimension of human psychology.

Complicated Grieving

For a long time, a distinction was drawn between "normal" and "abnormal" grief. However, that approach has long since been criticized because it is judgmental and stigmatizing. It implies that some people grieve in a pathological way, as if they have some sort of deficit or inadequacy. The reality, in fact, is far more complicated than this. As noted above, different people grieve in different ways, and so it is possible—indeed, it happens very often—that someone is grieving in a way that is not at all problematic but, because it is different from what some other people may expect, it may be perceived as a problem or as "abnormal." This is not to say that problematic grieving does not occur. It is unfortunately the case that some people have additional difficulties in terms of grieving, and these days this tends to be referred to as "complicated" grieving. Neimeyer captures the point well when he argues that:

> Although it is important not to "pathologize" grieving by presenting it as if it were an illness, it is also important to acknowledge that satisfactory reorganization of one's life following a major loss is not a guaranteed outcome. Indeed, there are several ways in which we can become "stuck" in the grief cycle, so that grieving is apparently absent, becomes chronic, or is

life-threatening. These negative outcomes may be more likely when the loss is a traumatic one (involving violation [of] one's own body, as in rape or physical assault; or a loved one is victimized by violence or senseless killing, as by a drunk driver). [6, p. 14]

It is important, but not always easy, to be able to differentiate between what is an expected grief reaction and, while painful and difficult, is not necessarily a sign that grieving is "going wrong," and "complicated" grieving in which help is likely to be needed to aid the person concerned in dealing with the problems being experienced. If we are not aware of the need for such a distinction, the result can be either a situation in which "normal" grieving is causing unnecessary concerns or one in which very real concerns are being missed. Both of these can be highly problematic and potentially harmful situations that are best avoided by a sensitivity to this important distinction.

This brief discussion of complicated grieving should be sufficient to show that, in supporting grieving employees, part of what we will need to consider is whether the thoughts, feelings and actions of the individual(s) concerned fall within the parameters of expected grief reactions (broadly defined) or are, by contrast, in some way problematic above and beyond the challenges that grief always presents. This is not so that we can put some people in the category of "poor coper" or some other such unhelpful schema, but rather to recognize in a positive and supportive who may need additional help or guidance.

Disenfranchised Grief

Another important aspect of grief to take into consideration is that of disenfranchised grief. A term introduced in the work of Kenneth Doka [7, 8], this significant concept can be summarized as follows:

Experiences of grief can be disenfranchised in the following ways:

- *The griever is disenfranchised.* Some people are often assumed not to grieve (for example, people with learning disabilities— "They don't understand") or to be used to grieving (for example, older people . . .). The people in these categories of disenfranchisement may therefore have their grief go unrecognized, because of stereotypical assumptions.
- *The relationship is disenfranchised.* Some forms of relationship are subject to social disapproval, in some quarters at least—gay relationships, for example. The break up of a long-standing relationship can be painful enough when that relationship is openly acknowledged, but where the relationship is a socially stigmatized one or a secret one (where one or both partners is married, but not to the other), the lack of openness, social support and/or comforting rituals can add significantly to the difficulties experienced.
- *The loss itself is disenfranchised.* Some forms of loss are, in themselves, disenfranchised. For example, the loss associated with perinatal deaths has been known to receive far less attention and recognition than other

deaths of infants. In addition, many losses that are not death-related
may be disenfranchised because of the strong tendency to associate loss
primarily with death. The losses involved in adoption would be a good
example of this. [9, p. 8]

Disenfranchised grief can make a significant loss even more difficult to deal
with as a result of the stigma and/or lack of social support that can accompany
such grief. This can apply just as much in the workplace as outside it. What can
compound matters perhaps to a dangerous extent is a workplace culture that can be
characterized by a lack of support and sensitivity—one where the idea that
employees should leave home issues outside of the work setting is prevalent.
Such an unrealistic and uncaring culture can therefore make a major contribution
to rendering workplace grief as disenfranchised grief, with all the potential
problems this entails.

Mourning: Grieving Together

Grieving is in some ways very personal and intimate, and can therefore be an
isolated activity, but that is only part of the story. There is also the dimension of
collective grieving, whether this is across a whole society, a sub-section of a
society, or a family or group of friends or, indeed, work colleagues. Some people
distinguish between "grieving," which tends to refer to the individual side of a
reaction to a loss and: "mourning," which is used to signify the social aspects of
responding to loss (rituals, shared expressions of grief and so on). Mourning or
grieving together can be mutually supportive, but it can also be divisive—for
example, Riches and Dawson [10], have undertaken important research work
about familial responses to the death of a child. One sad but significant fact that
emerges from their work is that the break-up rate for marriages following the death
of a child is significantly higher than the average. It is as if the parents grieve in
ways that lead to conflict where one partner does not recognize and support the
grieving style of the other. This phenomenon could also be seen to apply to the
workplace where a group of people who share a sense of grief as the result, for
example, of the death of a colleague, may find that they are subject to considerable
conflict as a consequence of the highly charged emotions leading to a tense
atmosphere in which different approaches to grieving can lead to conflict and
division.

Grief and Health

There is unfortunately a tendency for grief to be treated as an illness in some
quarters. It is not uncommon for people to talk of, for example, "symptoms" of
grief, but this can be very misleading. Although grief can exacerbate existing
illnesses (for example, the stress involved in a grief reaction may adversely affect
somebody with a heart condition) and grief can also, as we, noted above, result in
physical reactions, such as stomach aches or headaches, it is nonetheless the case

that grief is not an illness in itself. As we have seen, grief is our *psychological* response to loss. People often speak of "healing" in relation to grief, but it is important to understand that this term needs to be used in a metaphorical or spiritual sense, rather than in a literal, medical sense. When used appropriately, it can be a helpful term to characterize the process involved in "coming to terms with" a loss (although it has to be acknowledged that we may never completely come to terms with a major loss).

We should not, then, fall into the trap of seeing grief as an illness, and especially not as a mental illness. For example, the work of Schneider [11] has emphasized the dangers of confusing grief with depression. While grief can involve elements of depression, in the sense of low mood, grief, and depression are two very different phenomena:

> When you are grieving, you know there is a connection—you are struggling with how to recognize and embrace it, how to remember it and restore its meaning. To call what you are feeling "grief" powerfully validates, makes real, your loss, your grief and your power to transform it.
>
> When you grieve, you become aware of how profound your sense of loss is when those connections are disrupted. Honoring the fullness of your loss permits you to realize that you can't make it on your own, and you discover the delicate, essential threads of meaning and love, what I have called "gossamer threads," that still weave themselves through our life.
>
> Depression, conversely, implies a hopelessness—when what was once tangible is gone, nothing is left. Depression is something to survive, to cope with, or to defend against, but it is not a condition in which you can learn new ways or transform old ones. [11, p. 7]

Just as it is important to maintain the distinction between patterns of grief that are to be expected and "complicated" or problematic grief, it is imperative that we understand the differences between grieving and being depressed.

Practice Focus 1.2

After Kate's death, Lyn found life very difficult. She was experiencing all four sets of reactions (physical, emotional, cognitive and behavioral): she felt physically sick; her feelings of grief were quite acute, she was finding it difficult to concentrate, and all she wanted to do was withdraw into her own world. The loss of her sister had clearly had a profound effect on her.

She was having difficulty sleeping, and so she went to see her doctor to ask for sleeping tablets. However, without enquiring about Lyn's personal or social circumstances, the doctor assumed that she was depressed and proposed prescribing anti-depressant medication. Lyn was quite taken aback by this, as she knew she was not depressed; she was grieving and wanted help with her sleep difficulties. She was therefore quite vehement in rejecting her doctor's suggestion and went away feeling worse because she felt she had not been understood or supported in her hour of need. Her doctor, she felt, was too keen to pigeonhole her and did not take the trouble to find out what was really ailing her.

Schneider's work is very relevant in casting light on Lyn's situation (Practice Focus 1.2). He makes the important observation that:

> To be called "depressed" by a healthcare professional when you are grieving actually adds insult to injury. . . . Grieving doesn't mean you will get over or forget your loss; it means you have the potential to find the resources to get through it and be transformed by it. [11, p. 8]

Grieving in Stages

Another common misunderstanding of grief, and one that has been perpetuated by the continuing adherence to outdated theory, is the idea that people grieve in stages. There is now a convincing body of theoretical research evidence to confirm that, despite the predominance of this idea, people do not grieve in stages:

> Much of what we know about the human response to loss derives from adults who have lost a loved one through death. At least in these cases of profound and irretrievable loss, there appear to be certain common reactions, feelings, and processes of healing for those who are bereaved, although there are also important variations among mourners as a result of who they are, how they typically cope with adversity, and the nature of their relationship to the deceased individual. For this reason, it is misleading to speak of "stages" of grieving, as if all mourners follow the same path in their journey from painful separation to personal restoration. [7, p. 5]

We now have a far wider range of theoretical understandings of grief that are much more sophisticated than the simplistic notion that people grieve in stages. For example, there is the dual process theory of Stroebe and Schut [12] which argues that people will focus on the past and what they have lost as part of their grieving process, but will also focus on the future and what they have to rebuild. They further argue these two processes (looking back and looking forward) involve a degree of oscillation—that is, swinging backwards and forwards—between the two. In addition, there is the important theoretical work of Neimeyer and his colleagues which presents grieving as a process of "meaning reconstruction" [13, 14]. This involves having to develop a new "narrative" or story to make sense of our lives without the person, thing or relationship that we have lost.

These are much more helpful approaches to understanding the complexities of grief and have been significant in moving us away from the dangers of thinking that grieving is a simple, straightforward, albeit painful, process from one stage to the next and out the other end again.

Transformational Grief

Grief can also be "transformational." This means that, although the process of grieving may be a very painful one, the outcome can be a positive one. People can grow and develop and become strengthened by the experience of coping with a loss. This is more than the simple idea that the cloud of grief has a silver lining. It is about taking account of the fact that grief can be a major life challenge and, in rising to that challenge, we can become stronger—perhaps better prepared for the next challenge life will throw at us. For example, whether an individual is religious or not, he or she may feel spiritually better equipped to deal with life in the future than was the case before a loss. Calhoun and Tedeschi capture the point when they argue that:

> Crises can impair or destroy relationships. However, a consistent finding in the research on posttraumatic growth is that a significant number of persons report a strengthening of their relationships with others. The positive change is reflected in an experience of increased intimacy and closeness. [15, p. 11]

A crisis is a turning point in someone's life, an event that produces a situation that will either get better or get worse, but will not stay the same. It is the crucial moment at which normal equilibrium breaks down—the point where we cannot go on as before. Significant losses (and, as we shall see in Chapter 3, experiences of trauma) are forms of crisis.

What we have known about crises for some time now (see, for example, Thompson [16]) is that they can have positive or negative outcomes—that is, things can get better or they can get worse as a result of a crisis occurring. This logic can be applied to experience of loss. The grief generated by the loss can bring about a positive outcome alongside the painful feelings involved. Such positive developments can include:

- *Appreciation.* In the hurly burly of everyday life it is very easy to get drawn into the pressures of workaday life and lose sight of what is important to us: people, places, activities, values and so on. Experiencing a major loss can bring us down to earth with a bump, but, while that can be a painful and discomfiting experience, it can also help us become more fully aware of what we have going for us. That is, to lose an important person or thing can help us appreciate the ones we have not lost.
- *Stronger relationships.* As the quotation from Calhoun and Tedeschi above shows, relationships can be greatly enhanced by a major loss—it is as if we are reaffirming our remaining relationships after an important relationship has been transformed by death (or other loss). For some people this may be only a short-term gain, in the sense that, after a while, they return to their former state. However, for very many people, the benefits of strengthened relationships can be very long lasting indeed.

- *Resilience.* This refers to a person's ability to "bounce back" from adversity, to reestablish their equilibrium, possibly at a higher level of functioning than before. Resilience can help to deal with loss and grief situations, but the experience of loss can also boost resilience, thus producing a positive outcome from a negative situation.
- *Mental and emotional preparedness.* After experiencing a loss, an individual can feel better prepared for dealing with any future losses that arise, having the experience of the previous loss to draw on. This will not automatically happen, but the potential for positive learning is nonetheless there.
- *New vistas.* The breakdown of equilibrium (or "homeostasis," to use the technical term) can be extremely painful and disruptive, but it can also enable us to see situations in a new light, broaden our perspective and develop a new view of our life. For example, many people have developed new careers (entering the caring professions, perhaps) because their outlook on their working life has been changed as a result of loss.
- *Discovering new skills and talents.* The demands of a bereavement (or, indeed, other such crisis) can place a lot of pressure on us, but these can bring the best out in us (as adversity often does). For example, someone who has always tended to avoid emotional issues and has felt uncomfortable in dealing with them may, as a result of going through the emotional maelstrom of grief, learn to address emotional issues more confidently. It can be a matter of learning the hard way, but it can still be very valuable learning.
- *Life review.* A significant loss can be so disruptive to our sense of normality that we may take the opportunity to take stock of our lives, to review where we are up to and where we might see ourselves going in the new, transformed future that has arisen from the loss. This can be an important part of spirituality, helping us realize what is important and meaningful to us. As such, it can form the basis of making important, perhaps life-altering decisions, that can bring very positive change.
- *Wisdom to pass on.* While there are clearly positive benefits for ourselves as a result of the transformative potential of grief, the experience can also put us in a stronger position to support others through the difficulties. While no two people will grieve in exactly the same way, it is nontheless the case that someone who has experience of one or more major losses may well be in a good position to help others deal with their loss challenges.

Echoing this theme of the positive potential of loss, Schneider again offers helpful comment when, in discussing the differences between grief and depression, he shows how there can be a positive, life-affirming side to grief:

> In the end, being incorrectly diagnosed as "depressed" is a devastating waste of human potential since grieving as opposed to depression is perhaps the

greatest source of wisdom, creativity and revitalization known to any society. Many great works of literature, music, art, and dance have been composed as expressions of grief. Major scientific discoveries have come about as an attempt to cure an illness that destroyed the life of a scientist's loved one. Powerful acts of reconciliation that change entire countries or regions come from people like Nelson Mandela, Mother Teresa, or Martin Luther King who have suffered enormous losses and have then transformed them into a deep compassion for living. [11, p. 9]

Grieving and Gender

Although grief has been defined as the psychological reaction to loss, this should not blind us to the fact that there is also a social basis. As noted earlier, the term "mourning" is often used to refer to the more social aspects of grief. This includes rituals and other social processes by which a loss is recognized and dealt with. This is important, because it would be foolish not to take account of the fact that losses occur in a social context. There are many dimensions to this—for example, how people grieve will be strongly influenced by social and cultural patterns, the difference between, for example, how a Christian grieves and how a Sikh does so can be quite significant (see the *Guide to Further Learning* for more information about cultural differences). But it is not simply a matter of cultural or religious differences. For example, research has shown that there are significant gender differences in grieving. The work of Martin and Doka [17], for example, has shown that there are two gender-related styles of grieving: what can be called a masculine (or "instrumental") and a feminine (or "affective"). Feminine grieving is what has for many years been recognized as supposedly good or "healthy" grieving. It involves expressing emotion directly, talking about the loss, getting it off your chest, and so on. Martin and Doka's work has shown that most women and some men feel comfortable with this style of grieving. However, there is also the masculine style of grieving that is preferred by most men and some women. This style of grieving involves expressing emotion indirectly— for example, through actions. A man who is grieving may therefore prefer to mow the lawn twice as fast as he normally would, rather than sit and talk about his feelings of loss. For many years, this latter type of grieving was seen as a form of "abnormal" grief, but increasingly, we are understanding that it can be highly problematic to take such a simplistic view of some very complex issues. We need to look much more closely at how people are grieving and whether this is working for them in their particular way before we make any assessment as to whether the person concerned is experiencing difficulties in their grief.

If we are to accept that loss is a basic part of life, then so too must we accept that grief is central to human existence. It is therefore important to understand grief, to be prepared to support people through it and, where possible, help them grow and develop as a result of it (to make the grief "transformational"). A macho "just get over it and get on with your life" approach can be not only cruel and inhumane, it can also mean that opportunities for development are missed and that people are discouraged from the transformational potential of grief in the future. This can be an enormous waste of human potential—for both the individual concerned and his or her employers.

TRAUMA

A trauma can be defined as a psychological wound (although, as we noted above in relation to grief, a psychological emphasis does not rule out the significance of *social* understandings and interventions). The term is used by the medical profession to refer to physical wounds—but is also utilized in psychology and the caring professions to refer to a psychological wound—that is, the harm done to a person's psychological, spiritual and social well-being by one or more events that cause major levels of distress. Such events include:

- *Being seriously injured.* A serious physical trauma can be accompanied by a psychological trauma. For example, someone seriously injured in an automobile accident may develop a strong and debilitating phobia of motor travel.
- *Being assaulted, raped or robbed.* Victims of crime, particularly those crimes that involve violence and/or violation of the person or their home, can experience a strong traumatic reaction to such distressing incidents.
- *Experiencing a significant bereavement.* Any major loss can potentially lead to a traumatic reaction, but some losses are particularly likely to lead to trauma: an unexpected death (of a healthy child, for example); cumulative losses; multiple losses; and disenfranchised losses (as discussed above—for example, the death of a loved one by suicide).
- *Witnessing a death or major accident.* Even if the observer of such an event is not physically harmed in any way, psychological harm can very easily ensue in some cases. The impact of such an incident can be very powerful indeed.
- *Divorce or other significant relationship breakdown.* Relationships coming to an end can be very stressful events, but in some cases may even go so far as to produce a traumatic reaction—especially if there are other factors present that compound the situation (for example, more than one key relationship ending at the same time).
- *Experiencing a significant (non-death-related) loss or series of losses.* Losses associated with death are not the only ones that can produce traumatic results. A person who is made redundant from a job that he or she has held for over thirty years could be such a life-changing and destabilizing event as to lead to the experience of a trauma.
- *Being abused (physically, sexually or emotionally).* Abuse can undermine or even destroy dignity, self-respect, trust, confidence, security and well-being. It should not come as a surprise, then, to realize that abuse is a major

factor in the development of traumatic reactions. Such reactions can occur at the time of the abuse or shortly afterwards, but may also only materialize after some significant period of time—perhaps when another factor acts as a trigger.

Although a traumatic experience does not necessarily involve physical harm to the body, as with grief, physical symptoms can result—for example, headaches, stomach aches and/or palpitations. However, the psychological and social effects can be far more significant and far more damaging in both the short and long term.

Post-traumatic Stress Disorder

Trauma is very similar to loss, in the sense that it tends to produce a grief reaction. However, it is also significantly different, and so we must not make the mistake of oversimplifying the issues by regarding trauma as simply a subdivision of loss. One key difference is that trauma can lead to what is known as "post-traumatic stress disorder" (or PTSD for short), although we have to be careful that we do not rely on a medicalized approach to these issues that can run the risk of losing sight of the person. Returning to the point made earlier, that grief is not an illness, we can get ourselves into some very complex and unhelpful issues if we oversimplify the situation by regarding the psychological response involved in PTSD as simply an illness, as if it were some sort of disease. It is also important that we do not oversimplify these issues by confusing PTSD with post-traumatic stress more broadly. PTSD is used to refer to the situation when a person's post-traumatic stress reaction continues over time and is quite severe. It is the equivalent of complicated grieving and should not be equated with what is quite "normal" and healthy, which is the reaction of post-traumatic stress that people will generally show in the aftermath of a traumatic experience. Some degree of post-traumatic stress is a perfectly "normal" understandable reaction and does not necessarily mean that the individual concerned is in need of professional help. However, professionals are likely to have an important role to play if the problems persist over time (we shall return to this point in Chapter 3).

PTSD is often characterized by a number of factors, not least the following:

- *Flashbacks.* The distress can be relived over and over again—for example, when images, memories and associated emotions recur. This is sometimes in the form of vivid dreams, but is often just a matter of one's thoughts returning briefly to the scene.
- *Feelings of detachment.* Sometimes described as "emotional numbness," this involves feeling separated from the world and people around oneself. It can also involve feelings of low mood and pessimism.
- *Irritability.* Low levels of tolerance and increased "watchfulness" can lead to irritability, which can, in turn, affect sleep patterns and concentration.

A significant dimension of both post-traumatic stress, as a general reaction to trauma, and PTSD, as a particularly problematic reaction, is what is known as "intrusive thoughts." This refers to ideas that become quite obsessive and keep recurring (including flashbacks to the traumatic incident, as mentioned above). The effects of intrusive thoughts can be short term or long term, depending on the circumstances. Either way, we have to recognize that intrusive thoughts are likely to be a significant part of a trauma situation.

Practice Focus 1.3

Femi was trapped in a burning building when there was an explosion at the chemical works where he was employed. For the best part of an hour he was convinced that he was going to die, as he could see no way out and was aware that the fire was getting fiercer and spreading widely. He was therefore absolutely delighted when a team of firefighters managed to break through to where he was trapped and were able to get him out of the building before it collapsed or engulfed him in flames. However, despite this delight, the coming months were to be characterized by a strong traumatic reaction. He became very agitated at the slightest sign of tension or pressure. He would not enter buildings unless he had a clear exit available to him. This proved quite debilitating for him, but thankfully he grew more confident over time and gradually became less and less anxious, partly due to the professional support he had been receiving, but mainly to the strong backing he received from his employers and colleagues who made it clear they would support him all the way in getting over his experience.

While his progress was steady and very encouraging, one thing that persisted throughout this time and took much longer to die down was his tendency to have intrusive thoughts—for example, to have "flashbacks" to being trapped. He wondered how long this would go on for before he could put the incident behind him.

Helping People Who Have Been Traumatized

In terms of dealing with trauma, there are many forms of help available. For example, cognitive behavioral therapy (or CBT for short) is widely used, but there are other approaches, such as family therapy, that can also be drawn upon where appropriate. However, in addition to the important contribution professional help can make in many cases, considerable emphasis needs to be placed on the role of informal support, including that provided by work colleagues and others in the workplace—for example, a supportive line manager or human resources professional.

Trauma can happen anywhere, but the workplace in particular needs to be acknowledged as a potential site for trauma—especially when we consider how much of a person's waking time is spent at work. For example, as mentioned briefly above there may be a situation in which employees witness the death of a colleague, perhaps as a result of an industrial accident. There will also be situations where the effects of trauma outside of work can be carried over into the workplace (this will be discussed in more detail in Chapter 3). What can complicate matters further is the fact that trauma can apply to a group of people at the same time. For example, an organization affected by a terrorist attack may find itself in a situation where large numbers of their people are experiencing a trauma reaction. Trauma can therefore be a significant issue in the workplace and, equally, the workplace can be an important site of help (in terms of social support and maintaining a sense of normality and security, for example).

Secondary Trauma

There is also the phenomenon of "secondary traumatization" to consider. This refers to circumstances in which helpers (professional or voluntary) can have a traumatic reaction as a result of being involved in helping other people deal with a trauma—for example, in large-scale disasters—whether at the time of the key event or thereafter. This can include members of the emergency services and other relief workers (whether paid or voluntary) health care staff; social services staff, counselors and other such helpers, as well as relatives, friends and neighbors of the people directly affected by the trauma. Although some people may not be directly affected by the traumatic event, they may nonetheless experience a degree of trauma as a result of their exposure to the intense pain, distress and suffering involved.

We can see, then, that trauma is a psychological reaction, but is also linked to biological and social factors. It is a very complex field of study, and so trauma cannot simply be regarded as a mental illness in a biological sense. Nor is it something to be ashamed of. It is not the sign of a weak individual, although, unfortunately, some people can see it that way. Trauma presents society in general and the human services in particular with a set of quite demanding challenges. However, it is clear that these challenges have increased in significance in recent years as a result of the "war on terror" and the atrocities that led to its development. It is to the subject of terrorism that we now turn.

THE IMPLICATIONS OF TERRORISM

Terrorism is not a new phenomenon in the western world, but it is only in recent years that it has received the widespread concern and attention it currently attracts. While the very existence of terrorism is clearly a matter of major concern in terms of potential loss of life, serious injury and damage to property and personal and business assets, the term from which the concept derives its etymology—namely *terror*—is crucially important. Even if no actual death, injury or damage to property arises, there can nonetheless be extensive psychological and social damage caused by the persistence of fear. Indeed, terror goes beyond fear, as people can live with a degree of fear without it necessarily having any major adverse effect on their lives—the term "terror," however, implies a degree of reduction in level of functioning or even paralysis. It is for this reason that terror is associated with trauma—intense and prolonged fear of being harmed can in itself produce harm of a psychological nature. As we shall see in Chapter 3, this can have profound and far-reaching implications for the world of work.

The Danger of Panic

Terrorism has clearly been a major focus of concern since the tragic events of September 11ᵗʰ, 2001. This has produced a situation of heightened awareness of terrorism and the threat it poses. This in turn has produced, to some degree at least, a heightened awareness of loss, grief and trauma. However, it has not necessarily produced a heightened level of understanding to match the level of concern. The result of this is a very real danger of panic and overreaction, which in themselves can lead to unnecessary suffering. It is therefore important to recognize that, the higher the level of awareness of terrorism, the greater the need for an adequate understanding of loss, grief and trauma and how they need to be dealt with in situations involving a terrorist threat.

Practice Focus 1.4

Warren was a calm and level-headed manager. However, following an incident in which the building next store was evacuated as a result of a bomb scare, he found it very difficult to keep his team of staff calm and focused on the job. The office became a place characterized by high levels of tension, and the possibility of a terrorist attack was a constant topic of conversation. He was very concerned about this, particularly when he noticed the situation was escalating—the more anxious people got, the more concerned with the issue they became. He realized that the levels of tension were steadily rising and he feared that the whole situation was in danger of getting out of hand. He could not afford to let this happen, especially as much of the work the team were involved with required a great deal of concentration and attention to detail. He therefore decided to hold a meeting to give staff the opportunity to air their concerns and to give himself the opportunity to reassure them and point out the dangers of allowing feelings to overheat. This proved to be a good plan, but Warren realized he would need to keep a close eye on the situation and handle it very carefully. He wished he had a fuller understanding of how to deal with potential or actual crises and wondered whether he could receive some training on the subject.

The role of the media is a significant factor in this. It is understandable that terrorist-related stories are considered highly newsworthy, but the price we pay for such matters having a high profile is a significant contribution to "upping the stakes" in terms of tension levels. Being vigilant is an important part of safeguarding against terrorist attacks, but hypervigilance and unnecessarily high levels of tension can, of course, be very counterproductive.

The Significance of Terrorism for Loss, Grief and Trauma

Practice Focus 1.4 describes a situation where there was no real terror threat, just a false alarm in the adjacent building, but even this situation was enough to cause concern in terms of the potential for panic and overreaction. In situations involving an actual terrorist crisis, the potential is, of course considerably higher. Where an incident does occur, many of the important issues discussed in this chapter will come to the fore: the significance of loss (loss of security, confidence and so on); the impact of grief (cognitive, emotional and behavioral reactions to the losses involved); and the potential for trauma (as a result of exposure to extremes of fear). This means that the current emphasis on terrorism in the media and in public concerns makes it even more important that we have a good understanding of loss, grief and trauma—how to try and prevent them and how best to respond to them if or when they do arise.

CONCLUSION

In dealing with loss, grief and trauma, we are in fact working with highly complex issues. The fact that we encounter a strong tendency to avoid them, to deny that they are part of human existence adds to the complications. When we further add a tendency to oversimplify the issues when we do address them, the result is a very unsatisfactory state of affairs—indeed, a very *dangerous* state of affairs, when we consider just how far loss, grief and trauma impact on the workplace. The significance of this should become much clearer as we look in more detail at these issues in the following chapters.

Chapter 1 has served as a basic foundation for developing an understanding of loss, grief and trauma and their significance. Subsequent chapters will now add to that foundation of understanding by developing both the breadth and depth of the subject matter. However, in addition to this, there is the *Guide to Further Learning* at the end of the book which makes reference to a wide range of important resources to draw upon.

REFERENCES

1. L. A. DeSpelder and A. L. Strickland, *The Last Dance: Encountering Death and Dying* (7th Edition), McGraw-Hill, New York, 2005.
2. H. Feifel, *New Meanings of Death,* McGraw-Hill, New York, 1977.

3. M. Lattanzi-Licht, Grief in the Workplace: Supporting the Grieving Employee, in *Living with Grief at Work, at School, at Workshop,* J. D. Davidson and K. J. Doka (eds.), Hospice Foundation of America, Brunner/Mazel, Washington, DC, 1999.

4. K. J. Doka, Memorialization, Ritual, and Public Tragedy, in *Living with Grief: Coping with Public Tragedy,* M. Lattanzi-Licht and K. J. Doka (eds.), Hospice Foundation of America, Brunner/Mazel, Washington, DC, 2003.

5. P. E. Irion, Ritual Responses to Death, in *Living with Grief at Work, at School, at Workshop,* J. D. Davidson and K. J. Doka (eds.), Hospice Foundation of America, Brunner/Mazel, Washington, DC, 1999.

6. R. A. Neimeyer, *Lessons of Loss: A Guide to Coping,* Center for the Study of Loss and Transition, Memphis, Tennessee, 2000.

7. K. J. Doka (ed.), *Disenfranchised Grief: Recognizing Hidden Sorrow,* Lexington, Lexington, Massachusetts, 1989.

8. K. J. Doka (ed.), *Disenfranchised Grief: New Directions, Challenges and Strategies for Practice,* Lexington, New York, 2001.

9. N. Thompson, Introduction, in *Loss and Grief: A Guide for Human Services Practitioners,* N. Thompson (ed.), Palgrave Macmillan, Basingstoke, United Kingdom, 2002.

10. G. Riches and P. Dawson, *An Intimate Loneliness: Supporting Bereaved Parents and Siblings,* Open University Press, Buckingham, United Kingdom, 2000.

11. J. Schneider, *The Overdiagnosis of Depression: Recognizing Grief and its Transformative Potential,* Seasons Press, Traverse City, Michigan, 2000.

12. M. Stroebe and H. Scout, The Dual Process Model of Coping with Bereavement: Rationale and Description, *Death Studies, 23*(3), 1999.

13. R. A. Neimeyer, *Meaning Reconstruction and the Experience of Loss,* R. A. Neimeyer (ed.), American Psychological Association, Washington, DC, 2001.

14. R. A. Neimeyer and A. Anderson, Meaning Reconstruction Theory, in *Loss and Grief: A Guide for Human Services Practitioners,* N. Thompson (ed.), Palgrave Macmillan, Basingstoke, United Kingdom, and New York, 2002.

15. L. G. Calhoun and R. G. Tedeschi, *Facilitating Posttraumatic Growth: A Clinician's Guide,* Lawrence Erlbaum Associates, Mahwah, New Jersey, 1999.

16. N. Thompson, *Crisis Intervention Revisited,* Pepar Publications, Birmingham, United Kingdom, 1991.

17. T. L. Martin and K. J. Doka, *Men Don't Cry . . . Women Do: Transcending Gender Stereotypes of Grief,* Brunner/Mazel, Philadelphia, Pennsylvania, 2000.

CHAPTER 2
Loss and Grief in the Workplace

This is the first of two chapters to build on the introductory materials presented in Chapter 1. In this chapter, we explore issues relating to loss and grief in the workplace, to be followed up by Chapter 3 which concentrates on trauma in the workplace. The aim of Chapter 2 is to highlight some of the important implications of loss and grief for managers, human resource professionals and others concerned with what is increasingly being referred to these days as "workplace well-being." Indeed, it is important to emphasize at this early stage that this subject matter is vitally important for all managers, insofar as every manager has some degree of responsibility for the well-being of their staff. Similarly, all human resource professionals need to be "tuned in" to matters relating to loss, grief, and trauma—it is not simply a matter for specialists, such as employee assistance program professionals or occupational health staff. This is because, as we shall see, loss, grief and trauma can (and often do) have profound effects on workplace issues. To try to tackle them without at least some basis of understanding or to avoid tackling them by adopting an ostrich approach (burying your head in the sand and hoping the issues will never come up) are both very unwise approaches— and both are potentially disastrous.

In part, Chapter 2 sets the scene for the more practice-focused chapters: Chapter 4 on the policy context; Chapter 5 about providing care and support; and Chapter 6, where we shall explore what helps and what hinders when it comes to promoting good practice in relation to loss, grief and trauma in the workplace. In order to work out how best to take the issues forward and to be aware of what pitfalls to avoid in doing so, we need at least a basic foundation of understanding of the range of issues involved. Chapter 2 provides much of that foundation specifically in relation to loss and grief in the workplace (with Chapter 3 covering trauma in the workplace), and is supplemented by the *Guide to Further Learning* at the end of the book where guidance is provided about sources of additional information and learning as part of a process of building on the basis offered in this chapter.

A TYPOLOGY OF ORGANIZATIONS

In order to develop our understanding of these important issues, it can be helpful to consider how experiences of loss and grief (and their implications) apply to different types of organizations. This is because such matters will not apply across the board in a standard or uniform way. While some concerns will apply to *all* organizations, it is also the case that different organizations will face different challenges. The nature and focus of the organization can be significant in terms of key questions relating to the extent to which loss and grief issues feature and, indeed, how they can be dealt with. Furthermore, different organizations will be geared up in different ways when it comes to meeting the challenges presented by loss and grief. For example, all schools in which a child dies will face challenges of how to respond in a child-centered way that takes account of the development level of the children affected by the loss. However, how a faith school responds may be very different from how a secular school (or, indeed, a school representing a different faith) may deal with the situation.

In order to help understand the complexities involved, I want to outline a typology that divides organizations into four broad types. It is not intended that this should be an exhaustive or definitive schema, but rather, a helpful structure that can help us begin to develop our understanding of how the nature of an organization can shape how loss and grief issues arise and how they are dealt with. The four types are:

1. *Primary focus.* In organizations where loss and grief have a primary focus, death is likely to feature as a major part of the working week. Such organizations would include hospices, funeral homes and related organizations. In these settings, because death is a primary focus, loss issues feature in a highly significant way. Employees in such organizations may have had specialist training in dealing with the emotional pressures involved— although it is unfortunately the case that many will not have had the benefit of such training and will be left to cope as best they can in difficult circumstances. Such organizations will often develop their own rituals and coping methods for dealing with the intense and potentially painful subject matter of their work. Bartlett and Riches [1] provide an interesting discussion of how funeral directors manage the demands of their work in terms of the contrast between the somber outward appearance and the "behind the scenes" issues that will apply in any workplace. Similarly, Renzenbrink [2] offers an insightful discussion of the complex workplace dynamics that apply in hospice work.
2. *Central focus.* There will be a wide range of work settings where death is not a primary concern, but it is a central focus, in the sense that, while it may

not be a daily occurrence, it is nonetheless never far away. Such organizations would include some types of health care settings, the emergency services and, to a certain extent, care homes for older people. Here again, much will depend on whether staff have had appropriate training in responding appropriately to a death and, of equal importance, how to manage their own reactions to such a situation. There is evidence to suggest that practices in this regard vary widely, with some settings providing not only training, but also a supportive culture that enables people affected by a loss to receive the help and guidance they may need, while others adopt a much more guarded approach that can be not only unsupportive, but positively harmful. The work of Sidell, Katz and Komaromy [3] in relation to nursing homes is very instructive in this regard.

3. *Continuous focus.* This is a step down in the hierarchy, as it were, of degree of concern in relation to loss and grief issues. Here I am thinking primarily of social welfare organizations where death issues and, indeed, wider loss issues will continually appear as matters of concern, but are not a primary or central focus of the work. For example, a social worker working in a health care setting will not necessarily encounter death on a regular basis, but may well be working in an organization in which the potential for major loss is part and parcel of the work being undertaken—it is ever-present. Again, in such organizations there will be considerable variety in terms of training offered and the existence or otherwise of a supportive culture with helpful rituals that bring people together.

4. *Periodic focus.* This basically includes all other organizations, regardless of their size, nature, location or focus. *Any* organization will periodically face the challenge of loss and grief, for the simple reason that all organizations rely on people, and where there are people, sooner or later, there will be loss and grief. Such issues may arise as a result of a death or simply from the day-to-day nature of losses being brought into the organization or actually occurring within the organization—for example, as a result of a significant change initiative. It has long been recognized that, where there is change, there is loss, and where there is loss, there is change.

A basic typology such as this can provide us with a clear and helpful framework to make sense of the challenges we face in tackling loss and grief issues in the workplace. Perhaps the most important point that we can deduce from this typology is that it includes *all* organizations—no individual escapes death or loss, and the same can be said to apply to organizations. The challenge of dealing with loss and grief is not simply a matter for hospice workers, funeral directors, members of the emergency services, and so on. Any organization can and will face loss and grief issues. The question is not *whether* they will have to deal with such matters, but *when* and *how*.

One important implication of this typology is that it can be very helpful to work out where in this hierarchy a particular organization is located. For people offering consulting services it can be a useful analytical tool for beginning an assessment of how well geared up the organization in question is (how well equipped an organization is will depend on how significant the challenges it faces are, and this, in turn, will depend on where the organization falls within this typology).

For managers and human resource professionals (including EAP staff and occupational health professionals), it can be helpful to locate one's organization within this typology and then consider carefully what that may mean in relation to the demands of loss and grief in the world of work. It can provide a basis for addressing the following important questions:

- What risks are involved in relation to health and safety and, indeed, to employee well-being?
- Is training available for the staff (and managers) most at risk?
- Is there a supportive culture that faces up to the reality of loss and grief issues or is there a tendency to play denial games?
- Are there appropriate and helpful rituals established that enable people to recognize and honor a death or other significant loss?
- Are people in the organization aware of the dangers of failing to take loss and grief seriously?
- Are staff encouraged to practice self-care and to see needing help as a sign of strength rather than weakness?
- What steps need to be taken to rectify shortcomings and to build on existing strengths?
- Are there clear policies in place (see Chapter 4)?
- Are there clear lines of accountability for dealing with loss and grief, or is it simply left to the vagaries of how individuals choose to react at the time?

Practice Focus 2.1

Anna was an experienced manager from an industrial background who had had to deal with death-related issues on two separate occasions. However, when she became a manager at a large hospital, she quickly came to realize that death-related matters, while not exactly a day-to-day occurrence, were far more of a prominent concern in her new setting than they had been. It soon dawned on her that she had a steep learning curve ahead of her, as she remembered how difficult and challenging her two previous experiences of dealing with a death had been. When she also became aware that there were trauma issues to take into account in addition to death-related considerations, she recognized that she had her work cut out for her if she was to be able to remain a highly competent, effective and well-respected manager.

LOSS IN THE WORKPLACE

Loss can be seen to apply to the workplace in many different ways, some obvious, some not quite so apparent. An example of the latter would be the great extent of insecurity in modern (or indeed postmodern) workplaces. It has become increasingly clear that, with downsizing, downshifting and increased reliance on temporary contracts, contemporary workplaces are not the centers of stability and security that they once were. This has a range of implications that we shall explore in more detail below.

Workplace losses can be divided into two main categories: those relating to death and those not, and each of these can be further subdivided into losses that arise within the workplace and those that arise outside of the workplace but which can, nonetheless, have a significant impact on what goes on inside. It is worth exploring each of these in a little more detail.

Death-Related Losses

Death can arise anywhere and at any time, and the workplace is no exception to this. Death-related losses within the workplace would include:

- the death of one or more colleagues—for example, as the result of an accident or even homicide or suicide;
- individual deaths of clients, patients or others within the workplace—for example, as a consequence of a terminal illness;
- multiple deaths in the workplace as a result of a disaster (fire, explosion, avalanche, a mass shooting, and so on).

And, of course, it is sadly the case that, in this day and age, we need to add deaths as a result of terrorist attacks. We shall return to this point below.

Death can be significant *for* the workplace, even when it does not occur *in* the workplace. Death-related losses outside the workplace will of course include any death. This could be the death of a partner, a child, a friend, other family member, a neighbor or other significant person or persons. It is, of course, not possible for people to leave major losses outside when they turn up for work. While some degree of separation of work and wider aspects of life is to be expected, it would be naïve and unrealistic to expect one's reaction to a major loss to be "put on hold" while at work. Although many people find it helpful, even therapeutic up to a point, to immerse themselves in work tasks when they are grieving (as it helps to establish some sense of normality in a situation that is perhaps otherwise characterized by a high degree of insecurity and uncertainty), expecting events outside of work not to affect them is not an approach grounded in reality. While work tasks can certainly be experienced as a comforting counterbalance to a welter of confusion, there can still be problems if the significance of grief is not fully appreciated.

Other Losses

Losses within the workplace that are not death related include changes of role for specific individuals or, indeed, changes for a wide range of people as a result of a restructuring or a reconfiguration exercise within the organization. There can also be changes, and thus losses, on the arrival of a new manager who wishes to stake out his or her territory by bringing in changes in order to put his or her distinctive stamp on the way things work—what I like to refer to as the "tom cat" approach. Such a strategy by a new manager keen to make an impact can be very unwise, as it can result in (i) methods of work that were extremely effective being rejected; and (ii) considerable ill-feeling being generated among staff who resent having changes foisted upon them just to satisfy the empire-building tendencies and/or insecurities of a newly appointed manager. The net result of the tom cat approach can be an unnecessary additional layer of losses. Indeed, the significance of loss and grief as aspects of the change agenda in organizations raises significant and far-reaching questions for the whole discipline of change management. Stein makes an important point when he argues that:

> In workplace cultures and wider society, massive change and loss have become an increasingly menacing juggernaut when not followed by acknowledgment and acceptance of the loss and grieving for it. The triad of change-loss-grief looms ever larger in the face of recurrent and massive organizational change and globalization at the end of the 20th and into the 21st centuries. What Alexander and Margarete Mitserlich [4] called "the inability to mourn" often keeps organizations and entire societies 'stuck' in a repetition of the past and the inability to venture into a future that does not repeat it. [5, p. 98]

Whether the strategic management of the future will learn the lessons that an understanding of loss and grief brings remains to be seen.

Losses that are not death related from outside the workplace which may, nonetheless, have a significant impact within it would include: divorce or, in effect, the breakdown of any significant relationship in a person's life. Indeed, losses linked to the breakdown of a relationship can be enormously stressful and quite overwhelming—bringing a powerful tide of grief, even if it may not be recognized as such.

There would also be other significant losses to consider—for example, a child growing up and leaving home. It is important not to trivialize such matters because, to a person not so affected, it can seem a relatively minor issue and, indeed a positive one to see a child successfully grow up and leave home, but for the parent(s) concerned, it can actually be a very painful and difficult process of "letting go" in some respects (or, to be more accurate, "maintaining a continuing bond in radically transformed circumstances"—see the discussion of "continuing bonds" on p. 36). We should therefore not underestimate the significance of this for people affected by it.

Terrorism can also bring losses that are not death related—for example, the loss of a sense of security as a result of the anxiety and fear that can be generated by a terrorist incident, whether directly experienced in person or indirectly through the media. Such matters can easily be carried through to the workplace, even if they do not arise there to begin with. And, when they emerge in the workplace, they may be strengthened by being reinforced by similar feelings expressed by colleagues—people's anxieties feed off each other, and there can be a danger of escalation, as we noted in Chapter 1.

We can see from this brief overview that there is indeed a wide range of losses that can affect people in the workplace. What this overview also shows is the need to recognize: (i) that it is unrealistic to expect people to "switch off" from losses outside the workplace— life is not that simple; and (ii) that the workplace can create losses, sometimes when it is unnecessary and unhelpful to do so. This latter point reinforces the argument I put forward at the beginning of the chapter, namely, that managers and human resource professionals have important responsibilities in relation to how loss issues are managed at work in order to make sure that they do not cause unnecessary problems or do more harm than is necessary. This is part of the need for a fundamental commitment to promoting workplace well-being.

Practice Focus 2.2

Marisa was understandably devastated by the death of her husband, but she was keen to get back to work as soon as she could, as she felt that re-establishing as much normality as possible would help her cope with her intense feelings of grief she was experiencing. However, things did not work out as well as she had hoped. While she did not expect her manager or work colleagues to "carry" her or put themselves out for her, she did take it as read that they would show some understanding of her circumstances and the painful process she was going through. What happened in reality was that she was expected to leave her grief at the factory gate and get on with her work as if nothing had happened. She found this both unrealistic as an expectation and heartless as a response to a grieving colleague. What added to her distress was that there were significant changes taking place at work, but little or no consideration was being given to the impact of the losses involved on the staff concerned. This added an extra layer of grief to what was already a very demanding situation for Marisa. The result was that she felt unable to remain in work and therefore took sick leave on the grounds of the stress she was experiencing. This then took away the positives she had wanted from maintaining as much normality as possible, and she also had the added pressures of feeling very angry about how she had been treated so shabbily by her employers. She wondered whether she would ever get back to full strength and move on with her life.

GRIEF

There are some important issues we need to recognize in relation to grief. First of all, despite the fact that so many organizations offer only a few days of bereavement leave, if that, grief is not a matter that is resolved within a few days. The effects of a significant loss can last for weeks, months, or even years. What is also important to take into account (based on dual process theory, as discussed in Chapter 1) is that individuals can oscillate between focusing on what they have lost (an orientation towards the past and the sense of emptiness it creates in the present) and focusing on reorganizing their lives after the significant loss (an orientation towards their future). It can be misleading, therefore, to assume that, because you have evidence that somebody is being very positive about their future, they have therefore "got over" a loss and are not experiencing any difficulties in relation to it. It may well be that you are seeing someone while they are in restoration orientation, but in private later that day, they may be experiencing loss orientation very intensely.

Relearning the World

Grieving involves developing a new "narrative," a new set of meanings that help us make sense of our lives and lead us through it. Attig develops this idea by writing of the importance of "relearning" the world after a major loss. He captures the idea well when he argues that:

> Learning our way in the world and then relearning when we are bereaved is not simply a cognitive matter of mastering ideas; it is not simply a cognitive matter of learning *that* the world is different because someone we care about has died. Instead, the learning and relearning involve investment of ourselves as whole persons, in all facets of our life all at once, as we learn *how* to be ourselves in the world before, and then relearn after someone we care about dies. Through such relearning we find and make ways of living with our emotions and struggle to reestablish self-confidence, self-esteem, and identity in a biography colored by loss. [6, pp. 13–14]

Attig also makes the important point that this relearning is not necessarily something we do alone—others can also play a part:

> No other person can grieve for us. The challenges are ours to meet. Yet, there is much that others can do for us as we relearn our worlds, find new places in our physical and social surroundings, learn how to continue to care about those who have died in their absence, and struggle to find new, meaningful, and hopeful directions for our life stories. [6, p. 23]

This raises some important questions about how the world of work can, and perhaps should, play a part in supporting staff through a difficult period:

- *What part does the workplace play in this?* How can managers and colleagues play a positive role in helping someone grieve and "relearn" their world (bearing in mind that such help is not only humane and supportive, but also in the interest of the organization—see the discussion below of workplace well-being)?
- *Is the workplace helping to develop a new and positive narrative after a significant loss (or set of losses)?* Work is an important part of most people's lives. There is therefore immense potential for work to play a very positive role in coping with a major loss.
- *Or is the workplace somehow hindering this or adding to the difficulties?* Practice Focus 2.2 is a good example of how an insensitive workplace can cause great problems.

Meaning in the Workplace

This idea of creating a new narrative or set of meanings through "relearning" touches on the important issue of spiritual intelligence in the workplace, a set of ideas that have emerged from the emphasis in recent years on emotional intelligence [7–9]. Thompson and Harrison explain it in the following terms:

> The notion of "spiritual intelligence" is a relatively new addition to our understanding of organisational life and the psychology of work. It refers to:
>
> > the intelligence with which we address problems of meaning and value, the intelligence with which we can place our actions and our lives in a wider, richer, meaning-giving context, the intelligence with which we can assess that one course of action or one life-path is more meaningful than another. [10, pp. 3–4]
>
> Parallel with the tendency for authors to refer to emotional intelligence as EQ, Zohar and Marshall use the shorthand of SQ to refer to spiritual intelligence. They argue that:
>
> > We use SQ to reach more fully towards the developed persons that we have the potential to be. Each of us forms a character through a combination of experience and vision, a tension between what we actually do and the bigger, better things we might do. [8, p. 14]
>
> In a sense, spiritual intelligence is a development of the logic of the philosophy of human resource management that has steadily displaced traditional approaches to personnel management. Human resource management (HRM) is based on the principle that an organisation's most valuable asset and most important resource is its people—its human resource. If we are to take this principle seriously, then its logical conclusion is that organisations should take the necessary steps to ensure that its employees are as fulfilled as possible in their work, so that their motivation and commitment are maximised. This in turn should play a part in maximising effectiveness, quality, productivity, working relations and so on—all important factors in developing a successful

organisation. In principle, then, spiritual intelligence should be a helpful thing for employing organisations to promote. [10, p. 2]

There is a growing recognition that a key part of an effective and successful workplace is an acknowledgment of the central role of meaning in people's lives. If work plays a positive part in helping people make their lives meaningful, then it is likely that work will be a positive experience, with all that this entails in terms of motivation, commitment, quality and quantity of work and job satisfaction. In these days of "postmodern" insecurity relating to work, as discussed earlier, issues of meaning making within a workplace become increasingly important.

Practice Focus 2.3

Frank was not sure what direction he wanted his career to go in when he completed his university education. Wary of becoming too deeply engaged in a particular type of work before he really knew what he wanted to do, instead of applying for permanent jobs, he registered with an employment agency. This gave him the opportunity to work in five different places in six months. He enjoyed the changes of scene and the opportunity to meet a lot of new people and to try out different types of work. However, he was disappointed that none of the jobs he undertook offered him any real satisfaction—none gave him any sense that he was doing anything meaningful or significant. What it did make him realize, though, was that he did need to find a type of employment that offered him more than a good salary and favorable working conditions. He would be happier doing a less-well paid job that he found meaningful than a more highly paid one that he found dispiriting.

Holding On

For a very long time, the established wisdom relating to grief was that people need to let go and move on. However, in recent years this notion has been challenged, and we have seen the development of what is known as the "continuing bonds thesis" [11]. This is a theoretical perspective that has gained a lot of support in the past decade among both academics and professionals. It is based on the idea that grieving needs to involve finding a way of keeping the person or thing we have lost firmly in our lives. For example, while we may clearly know that a deceased person is no longer with us in a physical sense, rather than allow this physical absence to predominate in terms of our psychological and social lifeworlds, the opposite can apply, namely that we make every reasonable effort to keep that person as part of our lives in terms of what they have meant to us in the past and what they continue to mean to us in the present day. If someone has acted as a significant mentor and influence, then that influence can continue to apply, even though that person may no longer be physically with us. In this respect, the bond continues, the meaning continues. It is therefore dangerous to rely on dogmas that insist that we should "let go," however well-established and long-standing they may be.

The Role of Rituals

In Chapter 1, the significance of rituals was mentioned. It can be very important to honor and provide rituals for grief issues to be managed effectively and sensitively in the workplace. The importance of rituals should not be underestimated. As Doka comments:

> By doing something, even engaging in ritual, we feel that we have symbolic mastery over events. Ritual allows a reorganization of community and continuity in a chaotic time. Collectively, it offers a reassurance that while we cannot control the tragedy itself, we have reasserted control in its aftermath. [12, p. 180]

Where people wish to carry out a particular ritual in the workplace, unless this has health and safety or other such significant implications, its use should not be discouraged or forbidden. In certain circumstances, it may be necessary, or at least helpful and appropriate, for the workplace to provide an appropriate ritual of its own to develop some way of recognizing and honoring a significant loss, and thus bringing people together in terms of dealing with the implications. For example, some nursing homes light a candle in the entrance hall when someone has died, so that anyone arriving (including staff coming on duty) becomes aware of the situation on entering the building.

This sort of approach, however, can easily be sabotaged by an unhelpful tendency to brush loss issues under the carpet and pretend that they are not important. This can be a very dangerous tactic, even though it is perhaps understandable that many people brought up in a society that largely denies or underplays the significance of death [13] will find it difficult to address death-related issues head on. It is nonetheless a difficulty that needs to be overcome if workplace well-being is to be more than a tokenistic phrase.

Rituals can be of various kinds, but there are two particular types worth mentioning. One is a ritual of transition. This is a way of marking a transition from a position where someone or something was a part of somebody's life in a very direct and physical way to a new phase of life where that person or thing may well continue to be an important part of life, but not in a direct and physical way (see the discussion of continuing bonds, on p. 36). A funeral, for example, is a clear instance of a ritual of transition—a formal way of bringing people together to acknowledge the fact of transition from one set of circumstances to another.

The other key type of ritual is a ritual of continuity. This involves continuing to act in a particular way, even after a significant loss. A common example of this is where someone dies, but their belongings continue to remain in place thereafter—for example, parents who have lost a child may keep the child's bedroom almost as a type of shrine for a very long period of time so that, although their child may no longer be physically with them, symbolically his or her role in their emotional lives continues. In some respects, that is a relatively extreme example (although not uncommon). Other rituals of continuity that are perhaps not quite so extreme could include somebody who is divorced continuing to wear their wedding ring, almost as if to symbolize that the relationship is still meaningful to them, even though it is legally over.

Corporate Responsibility

In terms of rising to the challenge of grief in a workplace, it is vitally important that we recognize that it is not simply a matter of referral to an employee assistance program (EAP). Gilbert provides an excellent example of this when he describes his experience of becoming a senior manager for a social services organization:

> Visiting residential homes and day centers, I found a great many temporary staff in post. Front-line managers complained that, when people went off sick for physical or emotional reasons, there was no system for following them up and both expressing care and compassion, but also striving to get people back into the workplace as soon as was proper and practicable. There was no active human resources function, nor a counseling service linked to positive management practice. One member of staff in a home for older people had, in fact, been off sick for six years! There was no connection between the service and those people who were off sick through illness, loss, depression, and so on. When we did sort out an appropriate human resources system and set up a counseling service, one team manager suggested to me at a meeting, that any emotional issues in his team could be referred straight to the counselor! "No!" I replied, "that's your job!" [14, p. 220]

This brings us back to the important point that workplace well-being issues in general, and those relating to loss and grief in particular are not matters reserved for specialists. They are part and parcel of good people management practices.

The Challenge of Grief in the Workplace

These various points about the significance of grief should have helped to paint a picture once again of just how complex grief is, and therefore how seriously we need to take it if we are to play an important role in making the workplace as humane and effective a place of industry as possible. As was emphasized in the Introduction, work is important for the people who undertake it and for the organizations who invest their resources in providing work opportunities for their employees. Grief can be destructive for both the individual worker and for the organization more broadly (including its various stakeholders, such as customers or clients), but it can also be a positive contribution to drawing on the humanity of a place where people come together with shared goals, to a certain extent. A simplistic approach to grief can not only exacerbate the potential problems, but also miss out on the excellent opportunities in terms of personal growth, development and transformation. As Harvey puts it "Both loss and trauma spin us into dark woods. They are assaults against the self that diminish us but that sometimes help us grow and give back to others" [15, p. 1].

COMPLICATIONS IN GRIEVING

Grieving is generally a complex, difficult and painful process. However, it can sometimes go beyond this to become a problematic process, in the sense that grief is somehow "going wrong." Here I wish to sketch out a few brief examples of how this can occur so that we have a foundation from which to consider how best to respond to such issues. A well-informed approach to workplace grief will need to incorporate not only where grief follows an expected trajectory (a painful trajectory, of course, but one involving gradual "healing"), but also those situations where the trajectory is a highly problematic one.

Disenfranchised Grief

This is a concept that was introduced in Chapter 1, and it refers to those types of grief that are somehow not socially sanctioned, perhaps because they are stigmatized in some way or because they do not fit in with dominant approaches to the idea of grief (what Kastenbaum and Aisenberg [16] refer to as the "death system" of a particular society). A significant example of disenfranchised grief would be suicide. Grieving the death of someone important to us can be difficult enough, but when that death is by suicide, then there can be many additional complications, not least a sense of shame and stigma (whether justified or not). In situations where a colleague commits suicide (or even indeed a client or patient), the implications can be significant terms of both breadth (how far reaching the effects can be) and depth (how hard hit the people so affected can be). We should therefore not underestimate the significance of a loss through suicide.

Disenfranchised grief can also apply to losses that are not death related. In fact, the tendency for loss to be so strongly associated with bereavement can mean that non-death-related losses in general are prone to a degree of disenfranchisement because they can so easily be overlooked. However, beyond this, there can be specific losses that are in some way not socially sanctioned, and therefore come under the heading of disenfranchised grief. An example of this would be a loss linked to change where the change is seen as a positive development—for example, a promotion. It can seem bizarre that somebody could have a grief reaction to being promoted but, if such promotion means losing a status and set of circumstances that one felt very familiar and comfortable with (for example, losing equal relationships with colleagues that now become relationships of hierarchy and dominance), can spell all sorts of complications.

Multiple Losses

Again, this can apply to deaths or other sets of losses. It is unfortunately the case that significant losses can occur at the same time. In the example of death-related losses, this could be as a result of a disaster—a plane crash or the collapse of a building would be significant examples here (see the discussion of terrorism below). Corr captures the point well:

> experiencing multiple deaths or losses in a traumatic encounter—especially when they occur simultaneously or in rapid succession as happened on 9/11—can produce a form of bereavement overload in which mourners find it difficult to sort out and work through their losses, grief reactions, and mourning processes for each individual tragedy. [17, p. 70]

Similarly, in terms of a loss not related to death, a divorce could generate not simply the loss of a relationship, but a whole host of other losses associated with that relationship. These could include the loss of:

- Identity, to a certain extent at least.
- Contacts—for example, with children of the marriage or other relatives or shared friends.
- Self-esteem—especially if either or both parties feel that the divorce was as a result of his or her failings in some way.
- Confidence in starting new relationships (once bitten twice shy).
- Financial security—divorce can leave both partners significantly worse off in monetary terms.

Again, we should not underestimate the significance of this, as non-death-related losses can often be just as significant in their impact as a bereavement. It would be a serious mistake to assume that they should occupy a secondary role.

Cumulative Losses

This is similar to the impact of multiple losses except, in the case, they do not occur all at the same time but, rather, one after the other, perhaps in rapid succession. For example, in circumstances where somebody's mother dies only to be followed shortly afterwards by the death of his or her father (as if he died of a broken heart) and perhaps then followed by the death of another key person in that individual's life, could add up to a situation where the individual concerned feels unable to cope—overwhelmed by blow after emotional blow. Perhaps if those losses had been spread out over two or three years, they could have been managed much more effectively, but when they come in relatively rapid succession, the result may be overwhelming, and that person may need much more help than would otherwise have been the case.

Unfinished Business

This refers to situations in which a relationship ends (through death or other circumstance) where there are issues that have not been resolved. Where this occurs, it can add extra pressure and significantly complicate the business of dealing with the emotional and other psychological consequences of the loss. For example, if somebody had a falling out with a colleague and then that colleague dies before the two of them had a chance to get over their conflict and re-establish harmonious working relationships, the impact of the loss may be much more significant than if the colleague had died with a clean slate, as it were.

These are just some of the ways in which grief can be complicated and thus become problematic. There is no set way of dealing with these. Each situation has to be dealt with carefully and sensitively on its own merits. However, having some understanding of how such matters can be complicated and problematic puts us in a much stronger position for dealing with the issues than a position of ignorance would do.

The Impact of Terrorism

Grief, it was noted in Chapter 1, is our reaction to loss. We have also noted that terrorism brings a range of losses, whether as a result of an actual attack or incident or simply through the fear, anxiety and distress that the *possibility* of such an incident can give rise to. In the case of both an actual and a potential incident, the media play a significant role in drawing attention to the situation and can thus unwittingly exacerbate the problems involved. Media coverage can, in turn, contribute to terrorism featuring as a topic of conversation, in the workplace and elsewhere.

Grief and terrorism can therefore be seen to be closely linked in some ways, insofar as terrorism is in many ways a source of grief. An adequate understanding of grief—and how to deal with it from an organizational point of view—therefore needs to incorporate a consideration of the potential significance of terrorism. This would include the following:

- Does your organization have a policy on how it would respond to a terrorist incident, whether an actual one or a "false alarm" or the general unease that terror threats generate?
- Do you have an employee assistance program that has suitably trained staff to deal with a terrorism-related crisis?
- Do you have contingency plans for how you would respond if your organization were directly or indirectly involved in a terrorist incident?
- Have key personnel been briefed on their responsibilities in such a situation?

It is to be hoped that terrorism will one day be a thing of the past, but this is unlikely to be for some time yet. It is therefore imperative that we are as prepared as we can be for the potential disruption that even a false alarm or thwarted terrorist attack can cause.

WORKPLACE WELL-BEING

For many years now it has been recognized that an organization's most important resource is its human resource—its people. This has been a mainstay in the development of modern human resource practices and the theories underpinning them. However, the tendency to treat this as just a relatively empty slogan and not actually draw out the full implications of it has unfortunately become quite a significant part of working life. The implications are in fact quite profound and far reaching. If people really are an organization's most important resource, then the issue of staff care and support or, as it is increasingly being referred to these days, "workplace well-being" becomes a major consideration, and one that we ignore at our peril. In a sense, a commitment to workplace well-being is a form of organizational "enlightened self-interest." The notion of enlightened self-interest arises from the work of the French thinker and writer, Voltaire (1712–1778), in the 18th century. It is based on the idea that, if we make sure that we look after the interests of other people, then this, in effect, serves our own self-interest because it puts us in a position where we are more likely to be helped, protected and supported by those people. Supporting others, then, is not simply a matter of selfless philanthropy; it is in fact more accurately a sensible and realistic way of meeting the challenges of being an individual in a social world.

To get the best outcomes involves not being entirely self-centered, nor entirely selfless (both extremes can be unhelpful) but, rather, finding the balance of enlightened self-interest in which our interests are served by serving others. This is an important philosophy that can apply to organizations in which it is increasingly being recognized that, if staff are treated in a humane and supportive way, they are more likely to be productive, effective and committed, and this then has very positive implications in terms of reducing the number of problems experienced and the very costly consequences that can arise from any such problems. Workplace well-being as a form of organizational enlightened self-interest therefore includes an emphasis on staff care and tackling the problems employees encounter. These would include:

- stress,
- bullying and harassment,
- conflict,
- drug/alcohol abuse and, of course,
- loss, grief and trauma.

The problems that can arise for the organization if issues of loss and grief are not handled effectively and appropriately, include the following:

- *(Prolonged) sickness absence.* Grieving is not automatically a basis for sick leave, but sometimes the pressures are so great that sickness absence understandably and legitimately arises. However, if organizations are not supportive of a grieving employee, their harsh attitude may result in a prolonging of sickness absence which can be harmful for both the individual and the organization.
- *Reduced quality and quantity of work.* It is understandable that, following a significant loss, a person's quality of work and overall productivity can dip. However, how far such a dip goes and how long it lasts will depend in part on how well supported the employee is. This therefore raises important issues for employing organizations.
- *Reduced confidence.* A grieving employee may be less prepared to take risks as a result of a reduced sense of security brought about in large part by the major loss they have suffered. Organizations may therefore need to handle such situations very carefully and sensitively, particularly in those types of job where success depends on a certain degree of risk taking. In certain circumstances, it may be necessary for someone to have a change of duties temporarily, or to be supported by another colleague to ensure that problems do not arise in terms of the employee not being able to carry out their duties to the level required of them.
- *Concentration and memory.* It was noted in Chapter 1 that there can be cognitive effects of grief. Somebody's ability to concentrate and to retain key issues in memory can be adversely affected by grief. Such issues may need to be taken into consideration in terms of allocation of work and the role of a supervisor in overseeing individuals.
- *Conflict.* Colleagues who are insensitive to the needs of a grieving person can create unnecessary tensions and lead to unhelpful conflicts. In extreme cases, this may actually result in aggression.
- *Tensions.* Similarly, where colleagues are dealing with someone who is grieving, if the matter is not handled with some degree of confidence arising from an informed approach to the issues, the result can be "walking on eggshells"—that is, a very tense and unhelpful situation where people do not know what to say or what to do. This can be very destructive for all concerned.
- *Offending traditions.* This is a matter of valuing diversity. People from particular cultures or other such traditions may need to grieve in a particular way (see the section on cultural diversity in the *Guide to Further Learning* at the end of the book). If this is not taken into consideration (out of a lack of awareness or out of a lack of commitment to valuing diversity) the results can be very negative and harmful.
- *Alcohol misuse.* While it is by no means certain that somebody who is grieving will rely on alcohol, there is sufficient research evidence to raise it as a potential concern that the increased incidence of alcohol use at times

of grieving or trauma is well recorded [18]. Where someone has a tendency to use alcohol to excess, this pre-existing problem may be exacerbated by a grief reaction. Employing organizations therefore need to be sensitive to such issues if the situation is not to go seriously wrong.

If employing organizations adopt a harsh attitude towards such matters—for example, by adopting a "pull yourself together" approach—a great deal of harm can be done to the individual and therefore indirectly to the organization and its various stakeholders.

There is therefore a significant challenge of leadership in terms of the need to create a culture that is appropriately sensitive to the needs of grieving employees, while also balancing these against the needs of the wider organization.

Practice Focus 2.4

After many years as a hospice volunteer in the early stages of her career, Jayne was interested in issues of loss and grief. When it came to writing a dissertation for her leadership course, she was therefore keen to focus on how an effective leader needed to develop appropriate staff support systems (and, just as importantly, to develop an appropriate *culture* of support) in relation to loss and grief issues. However, after reading a newspaper article about the stresses faced by frontline workers in disaster situations, she realized that she would also need to include consideration of trauma issues. She therefore set about learning as much as she could about loss, grief and trauma in general and their significance for the workplace in particular. She wanted to develop a good understanding of how a commitment to workplace well-being could and should incorporate these important issues.

CONCLUSION

Loss and grief present quite a challenge to modern workplaces. Failure to rise to that challenge has the potential to be disastrous. This can apply in obvious ways in terms of such matters as sickness absence, difficulties in relation to recruitment and retention, and matters of concern arising in connection with quality and quantity of work. However, there can be a wide range of other difficulties, some of which have been outlined in this chapter, but also many others that are perhaps less predictable because they arise in relation to a specific set of circumstances. Whatever range of problems we take into account, what is very clear is that it is highly dangerous not to take such matters into consideration and just leave them to chance.

There are also ethical considerations to take into account. For example, do employers in the twenty-first century, an age of increasing corporate social responsibility, wish to be placed in the same category as Victorian industrialists who regarded employees as simply cogs in the machine? The insights of modern leadership teach us a very different lesson in terms of how to produce win-win outcomes in relation to matters of industrial relations. A more sophisticated understanding of, and approach to, loss and grief is therefore called for. The remainder of the book will play a part in taking this forward, and the *Guide to Further Learning* will also support this by providing signposts to additional opportunities to learn about these important issues.

REFERENCES

1. R. Bartlett and G. Riches, Magic, Secrets and Grim Reality: Death Work and Boundary Management in the Role of the Funeral Director, *Illness, Crisis & Loss, 15*(3), 2007.
2. I. Renzenbrink, The Shadow Side of Hospice Care, *Illness, Crisis & Loss, 15*(3), 2007.
3. M. Sidell, J. S. Katz and C. Komaromy, The Case for Palliative Care in Residential and Nursing Homes, in *Death, Dying and Bereavement* (2nd Edition), D. Dickenson, M. Johnson and J. S. Katz (eds.), Sage, London, United Kingdom and Thousand Oaks, California, 2000.
4. A. Mitserlich and M. Mitserlich, *The Inability to Mourn: Principles of Collective Behavior,* Grove Press, New York, 1967.
5. H. J. Stein, *Insight and Imagination: A Study of Knowing and Not-Knowing in Organizational Life,* Universities of America Press, Lanham, Maryland, 2007.
6. T. Attig, *How We Grieve: Relearning the World,* Oxford University Press, Oxford, United Kingdom and New York, 1996.
7. B. Moss, Illness, Crisis and Loss, Towards a Spiritually Intelligent Workplace, *Illness, Crisis & Loss, 15*(3), 2007.
8. D. Zohar and I. Marshall, *SQ: Connecting with Our Spiritual Intelligence,* Bloomsbury, London, United Kingdom, 2000.
9. D. Zohar and I. Marshall, *Spiritual Capital: Wealth We Can Live By,* Bloomsbury, London, United Kingdom, 2004.
10. N. Thompson and R. Harrison, *The Intelligent Organisation,* Learning Curve Publishing, Wrexham, United Kingdom, 2003.
11. D. Klass, P. R. Silverman and S. Nickman (eds.), *Continuing Bonds: New Understandings of Grief,* Taylor and Francis, Washington, DC, 1996.
12. K. J. Doka, Memorialization, Ritual and Public Tragedy, in *Living with Grief: Coping with Public Tragedy,* M. Lattanzi-Licht and K. J. Doka (eds.), Hospice Foundation of America, Brunner/Mazel, Washington, DC, 2003.
13. P. Aries, *The Hour of Our Death,* Oxford University Press, Oxford, United Kingdom and New York, 1991.
14. P. Gilbert, Nobody Noticed: Leadership and Issues of Workplace Loss and Grief, *Illness, Crisis & Loss, 15*(3), 2007.
15. J. H. Harvey, *Perspectives on Loss and Trauma: Assaults on the Self,* Sage, Thousand Oaks, California, 2002.
16. R. Kastenbaum and R. Aisenberg, *The Psychology of Death,* Springer, New York, 1972.

17. C. Corr, Loss, Grief, and Trauma in Public Tragedy, in *Living with Grief: Coping with Public Tragedy,* M. Lattanzi-Licht and K. J. Doka (eds.), Hospice Foundation of America, Brunner/Mazel, Washington, DC, 2003.
18. S. H. Stewart, Alcohol Abuse in Individuals Exposed to Trauma: A Critical Review, *Psychological Bulletin, 120*(1), pp. 83-112, 1996.

CHAPTER 3
Trauma in the Workplace

This chapter complements Chapter 2 by exploring the significance of trauma issues for the workplace. It includes discussion of situations relating to individuals who have been traumatized (as a result of being threatened with violence, for example) and whole groups of people who may be traumatized (as may happen in the wake of a disaster, for example). The aim is to deepen and extend our understanding of such matters, particularly as they relate to the workplace, so that we will be in a better position to respond to them when a trauma occurs.

The chapter begins with a section entitled "Understanding Trauma" and this builds to a certain extent on the introductory discussions that featured in Chapter 1. Next comes a consideration of particular issues that relate to members of the helping professions, as these people are, to a certain extent often in the front line of dealing with traumatic incidents. This leads into a discussion of how trauma can arise within workplace settings, followed by a consideration of how matters relating to trauma can intrude upon the workplace.

This chapter also identifies a number of significant effects of trauma before exploring how we can deal with trauma situations as they manifest themselves in a work context. Finally, before drawing the chapter to a close, there is a brief discussion of the relationship between trauma and terrorism.

UNDERSTANDING TRAUMA

In Chapter 1 we noted that trauma is a psychological wound, something that can potentially leave a scar as a result of an experience that quite significantly overwhelms our ability to cope. Trauma is also a form of loss, and generally a very profound loss at that. Such a loss can be concrete, in the sense that we lose something tangible (such as our home in the event of a natural disaster, for example) or it can be abstract, in the sense of losing something that is perhaps just as important to us but not quite so concrete—for example, our sense of safety or security. Trauma involves a wound, but it is important to consider what precisely is wounded. It can be helpful to think of this in terms of our identity being wounded,

47

as a significant trauma can so easily have the effect of leaving a person feeling that his or her sense of self has been undermined, if not altogether destroyed. That is, we can be left feeling that we no longer know who we are because the trauma has had such a devastating effect on our taken-for-granted assumptions. A key part of our identity is our self-esteem or self-worth, how much we value ourselves. Trauma can have a very negative impact on a person's self-esteem, with very significant consequences in a variety of ways. Linked to this is our sense of confidence, and this can be shattered as a result of our security being taken away by the factors leading up to the trauma and the actual traumatic experience itself. For example, someone whose self-esteem has been damaged may lose their confidence to such an extent that they are unable to continue in their post, or may carry out their duties at a dangerously low level of competence.

Brewin [1, p. 8] shows that traumatic experiences are not uncommon:

> Who are the victims of trauma? The answer is "most of us." Surveys have been carried out in the United States to document the likelihood of a person experiencing or witnessing physical assaults, accidents, disasters, or other incidents involving the risk of death or serious injury. Generally, between 70 and 80 percent of people will experience one of these events over the course of a lifetime. [2]

There are at least three ways in which trauma can be linked to the workplace. First of all, for many people their actual work is likely to bring them into contact with people who have been traumatized in some way. This would include emergency services personnel, health workers and others involved in the human services. We shall return to this point below. Second, there will be traumatic events or incidents that occur within the workplace itself. No matter how careful or cautious employing organizations are, there is no guarantee that we can have workplaces that do not involve at some point some degree of trauma. Third, there will be events that occur outside the workplace that have the effect of "spilling over" into the world of work—that is, there will be everyday life experiences that have traumatic consequences that will have an impact on what goes on within the workplace.

In trying to understand how significant trauma is, it is important to recognize that it is a profoundly social occurrence. This can be seen to apply in at least three ways:

- *Interpersonal.* What affects one person is likely to affect a whole network of people. We are, of course, not isolated individuals, separate from other human beings. There will be significant ripple effects as a result of traumatic experiences. If we try to understand trauma in isolation from its impact on other people, then we will have a very distorted and partial picture, one that is going to be far from helpful in trying to develop systems and practices that can be of benefit in supporting people who have been traumatized in some way.

- *Cultural.* Culture is very relevant to trauma in a number of ways. For one, a person's psychological response to a traumatic situation will be very much of an individualized nature, but it will also reflect the wider cultural values and shared meanings that are part of the individual's background. As Bracken puts it: "traumatic experiences will effect different responses in individuals, depending on the culture in which they live" [3, p. 73]. Cultures will also have different ways of conceiving and responding to traumatic situations. Traumatic experiences can turn upside down our understanding of the world and cultural taken-for-granted assumptions and unwritten rules can be very significant in helping us to rebuild a sense of order and meaning in the aftermath of a trauma.
- *Structural.* Society is not a level playing field. It can be seen to be divided into different groups, with different levels of resources, power and life chances. These can be very significant at a time of trauma—for example, the resources that a person can draw upon in a traumatic situation or in the aftermath of one, will depend to a large extent on such things as where they fit into the socio-economic hierarchy. That is, while a rich person may be just as emotionally affected by a trauma as a poor person, the former may be able to draw on resources to "cushion the blow" that are not available to the latter.

Recognizing the social nature of trauma is consistent with the work of Bracken who argues that there are dangers involved in taking too individualistic or "atomistic" a view of what happens in a trauma situation:

> the current discourse on trauma is simply inadequate to grasp the complexity of how different human beings living in different cultures respond to terrifying events. There are problems with attempts to understand trauma as an event impacting on an individual in isolation, [and] problems with models of emotions that separate these from cultural context. [3, p. 80]

Similarly, Nash, Munford and O'Donoghue explain the importance of recognizing environmental factors that influence how a traumatic experience unfolds and how it affects the individuals concerned:

> The social and intellectual dominance of scientific knowledge has, however, had some disadvantages for work with the traumatized, in that it has constructed a short-sighted focus on the physical and behavioural aspects of traumatization and has underplayed the role that the environmental context has both in creating the trauma, and in our response to recovery from trauma. An ecological understanding suggests that the dynamic interaction between different levels of experience will influence any outcome of intervention. [4, p. 66]

Families are an important part of the social context and this is something that is recognized in the work of Nadeau [5] who writes of the significant role of what she refers to as "family storytelling." Such stories are an important resource in terms of recovering from trauma (the importance of story or "narrative" is a topic to which we shall return below). Work settings can be seen to be similar to families in some respects, and so there are important implications here in terms of how the workplace and the people within it can be a significant resource, and indeed influence, when it comes to an employee dealing with the aftermath of a trauma. This point is captured in the following passage from Gordon:

> In a very real sense in our society, the workplace has become a kind of extended family. Businesses have responded to the changing needs of American families by adding programs that reflect this connection between work and life, such as flexible work schedules, onsite childcare, and support for employees caring for aging parents or other loved ones. It follows, then that grief and bereavement issues affect a workplace as well. [6, p. ix]

Practice Focus 3.1

Ray and Pauline were devastated when their daughter, Nia, died following a tragic accident on a school outing. Both wanted to return to work as soon as they reasonably could to try and establish some sense of normality in these very trying circumstances. However, what they had not anticipated was the different response each of them received from their respective work settings. Ray was pleased that his colleagues and managers were very supportive and understanding. They gave him the opportunity to talk about his feelings when he wanted to and helped him to adjust to his new circumstances. It did not take away the pain, but it did help him make the transition. He therefore felt that returning to work was the right thing to do, as it helped him to begin to renew his sense of security that had been shattered by Nia's death. Pauline, by contrast, had a very different experience. Her colleagues and managers made a lot of sympathetic noises, but tended to shy away from her, as if they were frightened of opening the emotional floodgates. Pauline felt that she was a nuisance, disrupting the normal flow of work—a feeling that added to her distress and sense of trauma. Not only did she feel it was a mistake to return to work so soon, she also considered giving up her job, such was her disappointment at the response to the trauma she and Ray had experienced.

Trauma can be linked to stress, as a traumatic situation is by definition a stressful one—that is, one that overwhelms our coping resources at the time. This introduces a significant danger insofar as we have seen in recent years significant misunderstandings and oversimplifications in relation to stress—for example, the misguided notion that stress is necessarily the sign of a weak individual [7]. It is important that the problems we experience in relation to oversimplifying stress should not also be applied to trauma. If we are to be serious about tackling trauma issues in the workplace, then it is important that we do not lose sight of the complexities involved, and that we are prepared to build on our knowledge over time.

THE HELPING PROFESSIONS

As was mentioned earlier, when it comes to trauma in the workplace, there are certain groups of staff who are particularly exposed to the danger of trauma because of the nature of their work. These include the following:

- *Emergency services personnel.* Paramedics, firefighters, police officers and other ancillary staff are a primary group when it comes to being in the front line in relation to trauma. This has been clearly illustrated in relation to the events after 9/11.
- *Health care staff.* Doctors, nurses and other health care professionals will be called upon to deal not only with physical wounds, but also psychological traumas.
- *Other human services* This will include social workers, counselors and a variety of other people who are involved in some way in promoting social and personal well-being.

What all these professionals have in common is a professional disposition to what is known as secondary or vicarious traumatization. This refers to situations in which people who are trying to help those who have been affected by trauma can themselves experience the effects of the event as if the trauma had happened to them directly.

Friedman [8] discusses three aspects of this situation. The first refers to situations where helpers who have never actually been traumatized themselves become overwhelmed by the experiences they learn of through their efforts to help others. This can include nightmares, feelings of powerlessness and emotional numbness. He points out that this may lead to a vicious circle in which these negative experiences can reduce the effectiveness of the helper and thus lead to further problems.

The second aspect relates to circumstances in which dealing with someone else's trauma can trigger intrusive memories of traumatic experiences that the helper has encountered in their own life in the past. For example, someone assisting in responding to a road traffic accident may find that the experience opens up old wounds of a previous personal experience of almost being killed in such an accident (or losing a loved one in such circumstances).

The third aspect relates to situations in which people are trying to assist others in circumstances where they too have shared a traumatic experience—for example, a therapist working with someone traumatized by a natural disaster that also affected the therapist him- or herself.

To Friedman's list of three key issues we can add a fourth factor to consider, namely the significance of "survivor guilt." Cable and Martin give an example of this in relation to terrorism: "At the World Trade Center, some first responders experienced survivor guilt, which was exacerbated by their elevation to hero status by the press and public" [9, p. 80].

These four sets of circumstances raise important issues connected with implications of self-care measures, and so this is a point to which we shall return in Chapter 6, where the emphasis will be on providing care and support.

The point was made in Chapter 1 that trauma can influence the workplace in one of two ways, either by arising within the workplace itself or by being imported into the workplace by employees. We shall now explore each of these two sets of circumstances in a little more depth.

TRAUMATIC EVENTS IN THE WORKPLACE

In many ways, the workplace is a microcosm of wider society, in the sense that so much of what occurs *outside* the workplace is also mirrored *within* the workplace. Therefore work settings will feature, from time to time, a wide range of events and circumstances that can be actually or potentially traumatic for the people so affected. These include, but are not limited to, the following:

Industrial Accidents and Disablement

An emphasis on health and safety in the workplace has significantly reduced the number of accidents at work over the years, but it is important to recognize that the workplace still accounts for a large number of accidents, many of which have the result of bringing about some form of disablement. While accidents, even those that result in disablement, are not necessarily traumatic, they have huge potential to produce a traumatic reaction. This can apply in one of two ways: the person who becomes disabled may be traumatized by the event and/or anyone witnessing the event can experience a trauma reaction. It is a great irony in respect of how trauma works that there can be situations in which the person who is directly involved in the accident is not traumatized, while somebody witnessing the very same occurrence is. This illustrates how strong an element of subjectivity there is in the psychological experience of trauma. There is no single way of responding to such events.

Death

Bereavement in itself can produce a significant traumatic reaction, but so too can witnessing the death of a colleague or of any other person in the workplace. It is as if an encounter with death acts as a painful reminder of the finite nature of human existence and just how fragile and vulnerable we are as human beings. Of course, some workplaces will carry a higher risk of death than others—serving in the armed forces being an obvious example of this.

Death is part of life, but cultural attitudes towards the end of life can often leave us feeling ill equipped to deal with the challenges involved. As Kellehear tellingly comments:

> Often it seems to me as if one half of the modern world believes it will never die. Death is increasingly being greeted in wealthy countries and communities with more than mere shock or horror. Death is no longer a taboo subject but it is now commonly viewed as a great social rudeness. The violence and finality of death is an affront to everything we value—planning, certainty, cerebral abstractions and reliable help. [10, p. 162]

In such a context, death can be a significant source of trauma, due to its tendency to shatter our assumptions and understanding of life. While death continues not to be seen as a part of life, its trauma-inducing potential will remain higher than it needs to be.

Bullying and Harassment

It is unfortunately the case that bullying and harassment continue to be significant problems in modern workplaces despite efforts over the years to address these unwelcome aspects of working life [11-13]. There are very many cases on record of situations in which people have been bullied or harassed to such an extent that it has destroyed their confidence, undermined their sense of security and in so doing, hence produced a trauma situation.

Sexual and racial harassment are relatively well-known phenomena in the workplace, but we should also be aware that harassment can apply in addition to disability; sexual orientation; age; religion; language; and, indeed, any social difference that can form the basis of unfair discrimination. Each of these has the potential to establish a platform from which trauma can arise if the unfair treatment is sufficiently severe and/or prolonged.

Aggression and Violence

No workplace is immune from the potential for aggression and violence, but of course some workplaces are more likely to witness these problems than others. Where they do arise, they can leave a significant scar, not only on those directly affected by them, but also on those involved in bearing testimony to what has happened.

Violence, as the term itself indicates, implies a degree of violation. Feelings of violation can be a significant part of trauma, as these can leave someone feeling that their basis of security has been taken away from them. Incidences of violence in the workplace can therefore be of major significance in terms of the likely development of trauma reactions.

Practice Focus 3.2

Maria had no previous experience of working with people with develop-mental disabilities when she took up her post as a care assistant in a supported accommodation unit. She received no training or guidance in how to prevent or defuse aggression or how to handle violent situations if they arose. Her first few shifts on duty presented no difficulties as the residents were calm and relaxed and no tensions arose. However, after she had a day off she returned to work to find a new resident, Ella, had been admitted. Unbeknown to her, this resident had a history of violence. She was very pleasant while things were going her way, but could become violent if frustrated for any reason. No one told Maria of this. Less than an hour after starting her shift, she was assaulted by Ella following a confrontation between her and another resident. Maria was sitting at her desk, just about to make a phone call, when Ella approached her from behind, grabbed her by the hair and dragged her to the floor. She then started kicking her. Fortunately, another member of staff was on hand to intervene before serious injury was caused.

Maria was taken to the hospital, but was discharged later that day. Her employers were supportive of her in relation to the injuries but tried to absolve themselves of blame for the incident by trying to claim that Maria had brought the assault upon herself by handling the situation badly. This added insult to injury, and Maria was so traumatized by the incident itself and the untrustworthy response of her employers that she had to give up her job. She even started having panic attacks whenever she encountered someone with a developmental disability—for example, while out shopping. As a result of this, she commenced legal action against her former employers to seek compensation.

Sexual Abuse

While sexual harassment is no laughing matter [13], actual sexual violation is an even more significant problem in terms of the potential for a traumatic reaction. While sexual abuse is not an everyday occurrence in the workplace, it is sadly the case that incidences of rape and/or sexual assault do occur in work settings.

Some workplaces can, for various reasons, be sexually quite highly charged and thus lay the foundations for sexually abusive or exploitative relationships to develop. However, even workplaces with no sexual charge *per se* are not immune from such problems.

Crime

Being a victim of crime or a witness to a serious incident can also be traumatic. This is especially the case when such crimes involve some degree of violation or threat to security (armed robbery, for example). Particularly problematic can be crimes that involve kidnaping or hostage situations. A significant phenomenon that has arisen from such situations is what is known as the Stockholm syndrome. This refers to situations in which hostages form an attachment to their captors. In such circumstances, hostages can become supportive of the people who are in effect oppressing them at that moment. The term derives from an incident in Sweden in 1973 when bank employees were held hostage during a robbery. Surprisingly, the staff showed a degree of loyalty and affection towards the robbers and actually attempted to protect them from police fire when the robbers were under attack [14]. This shows how reactions to trauma can be quite extreme and out of character.

Terrorism

The comments above about kidnaping and hostage situations can also apply here, particularly in circumstances involving some form of hijack. However, it is important to recognize that terrorism can have a much broader effect on the workplace, whether through actual incidents of terror or through the behaviors that arise as a result of fear of a terrorist situation developing. For example, anxieties about terrorist incidents can lead to high levels of tension, poor concentration, increased error rates and so on. There is also the disruption that can be brought about by false alarms, such as a suspicious-looking package which later turns out to be entirely innocuous.

Clearly, then, there are various ways in which events in the workplace can contribute to the incidence of trauma in people's lives. This shows us that it would be unwise to neglect this aspect of working life. However, there is also the other side of the coin to consider, the various ways in which traumatic events that occur outside the workplace nonetheless have an impact within it. It is to these that we now turn.

TRAUMA ENTERS THE WORKPLACE

Work is a significant part of so many people's lives, but of course there are so many other aspects of our lives outside of work that it would be naïve to think that what happens outside of the workplace does not in some way impinge on what occurs within the four walls, as it were, of the working environment. It is therefore important to revisit the sets of circumstances outlined in the previous section that apply within the workplace and consider how issues relating to these from outside the workplace can, nonetheless, have a significant bearing.

Accidents and Disablement

While the workplace is a significant source of accidents, we need to be aware that the home is a much greater source of such occurrences and, indeed, there is also the wider sphere of, for example, the transport system—and the high rate of road traffic accidents—to consider. The effects of such accidents, particularly where they lead to some form of disablement, can therefore be quite significant. In many cases, such circumstances will have a direct effect on events within the workplace in terms of the behavior, attitudes and feelings of the individuals concerned.

Traumatic accidents can disrupt the workplace as a result of prolonged sickness absence and/or impaired working capability—whether the consequences of physical injury or a loss of confidence or both.

Death

The loss of a loved one can, of course, be a devastating occurrence. It can leave people feeling totally disorientated, unable to cope with their lives, including their working lives. This can be significant for the workplace in a number of ways. For example, it can result in prolonged absence from work as a result of the grief and/or any stress or exacerbation of medical problems arising from the situation. The situation can also be significant when people return to work before they are ready for it and may thus be performing at a level that falls below accepted standards and may actually be resulting in dangerous practice. Such situations have to be handled very carefully and sensitively.

Colleagues can also be affected if they know that the person concerned is deep in the thrall of grief and may feel awkward and uncomfortable in his or her presence, perhaps resulting in an adverse effect on quality and/or quantity of work (see Practice Focus 3.2).

Bullying and Harassment

While the topic of bullying and harassment is often strongly associated with the workplace, such unacceptable behaviors are not restricted to the workplace itself. People can be bullied or harassed in their private lives—for example, by neighbors, members of a club or society, or other members of their network. Even though the bullying or harassment may be taking place outside of work, the impact on the workplace can, at times, be just as great as in situations in which the events were occurring within the workplace itself.

For some people who are being bullied outside the workplace, work may be a potential source of solace or relief from the pressures and may thus be a positive experience for the person concerned. However, for others, the demeaning and demoralizing effects will be carried into the work setting, with potentially quite detrimental consequences.

Aggression and Violence

Being a victim of, or a witness to, aggression and violence is unfortunately an everyday possibility in the twenty-first century, in Western societies at least.

The psychological impact of this can be quite profound, and can have a bearing on how work duties are carried out. For example, someone who has been subject to aggression or violence outside of the workplace may feel unduly anxious about dealing with situations where the risk of aggression or violence is low but, as a result of their experiences, they are understandably being very cautious—if not overcautious.

If the aggression or violence is linked to domestic abuse, the problems may be ongoing, rather than limited to an isolated incident. This can raise some particularly sensitive challenges and thus some situations that will need to be handled very carefully.

Sexual Abuse

Herman [15] points out that, for men, the most likely cause of trauma is being involved in some sort of combat situation, whereas for women, the most likely cause of trauma is some form of sexual abuse. Despite the developments in sexual equality since the days of the Suffragettes, we clearly still have a long way to go when it comes to issues relating to women being respected and treated as human beings in their own right and not as simply sexual objects.

Although sexual violation is primarily a problem that affects women, we should not ignore the fact that some men will also experience some form of sexually abusive behavior—whether at the hands of women or other men. Anyone, then, can potentially be a recipient of sexual abuse.

Crime

Even in situations where no direct physical harm is caused, being the victim of a crime can nonetheless be quite traumatic. This is especially the case when a violation of one's home is involved. To a police officer, a burglary may be a relatively routine and mundane event, whereas, to the householder concerned, it could be an event that is extremely distressing and undermining. It is something that could leave a scar for a very long time, leaving those so affected feeling very insecure.

In addition to being a victim or a witness of crime, trauma can arise as a result of being "processed" as a criminal. This can refer to the shame and guilt that are felt when somebody is rightfully arrested and taken to court, or from the grave sense of injustice and acute embarrassment when somebody is inappropriately arrested and taken through the criminal justice system. This can apply to the person who is actually being "processed" or to close relatives or friends who may be concerned about his or her welfare.

Terrorism

The point has already been made that terrorism is a feature of our contemporary society. The dynamics of world politics acted out on the macro-level stage will no doubt continue to have an impact on micro-level interactions, both within the workplace and in the wider social sphere of each individual's personal family life and within our communities. While that continues to be the case, there will be anxieties that will inevitably feed into the workplace in different ways and at different times.

Practice Focus 3.3

Sam was delighted to get tickets to see his favourite rock band in concert. However, on the night of the concert, his joy was to turn to terror when a bomb scare at the concert venue led to a mass panic, resulting in many people receiving crush injuries. Fortunately no one was killed. Sam himself was injured, although not seriously. However, the fact that he thought he was going to die was enough to produce a traumatic reaction. Part of this was a profound fear of crowds, even relatively small gatherings of people. In effect, he became quite agoraphobic, with the result that his personal and social life became quite restricted. But it also had a profound effect on his working life. While he was able to do his basic desk-bound duties, anything that involved moving beyond his quite limited safety zone caused him major anxiety. The outcome of this was that his value to his employers dropped considerably after his exposure to trauma. It soon came to a head when his employers began to realize that there was something seriously wrong but they were not sure what it was. Whether his employers would support him through the difficulties or simply replace him with somebody more reliable became the key issue.

These are all important issues that have, as we have seen, a potentially significant bearing on the experience of trauma. However, there is one further set of issues that applies outside of the workplace which can bring with it a number of implications for what goes on within the workplace. I am referring to terminal illness. While a terminally ill person will continue to be terminally ill in the workplace, the development of a life-threatening illness is something that will affect the whole of their life. Someone who develops a terminal illness will clearly face huge challenges and those challenges will no doubt affect what happens in the workplace. It is important that we should not oversimplify and assume that anybody with such an illness will no longer be in the workplace as they will be on extended sick leave. What happens in very many cases is that people with life-threatening illnesses can continue to work for months, if not years, before they eventually pass away. This raises significant implications for how such matters should be dealt with. Tehan [16] provides an excellent example of the sort of scheme that can be developed in progressive workplaces to address these concerns effectively.

THE EFFECTS OF TRAUMA

If we are to have an adequate understanding of trauma to prepare us for dealing with it, then we need to understand not only the different arenas in which it can occur—whether within or outside the workplace—but also what effects trauma has on the individuals concerned and the wider constituency of people affected. In considering the effects of trauma, it is important to begin by reminding ourselves of just how significant a life experience trauma is. As Herman helpfully puts it:

> Traumatic events call into question basic human relationships. They breach the attachments of family, friendship, love and community. They shatter the construction of the self that is formed and sustained in relation to others. They undermine the belief systems that give meaning to human experience. They violate the victim's faith in a natural or divine order and cast the victim into an existential crisis. [15, p. 51]

In this regard, Bracken's comments are also instructive:

> there are times when the meaningfulness of the world is withdrawn— situations in which all the elements of our lives are still present but the background sense of coherence retreats. At these times it appears that the chequered board has been removed. The pieces remain in place but their connection to one another becomes arbitrary. These are times when we are confronted with the sense that there is no ground at all beneath our feet and our lives come to lack direction and purpose. [3, p. 1]

In Chapter 1, I pointed out that, while trauma is often referred to as an emotional reaction to an overwhelming event, it is perhaps best understood as a *psychological* (or, better still, a psychosocial) reaction, in the sense that it is not just feelings that are affected. The effects of trauma include: our thought processes, in terms of memory, concentration and reasoning; our emotions in terms of feelings being "frozen," or what is known as "dissociation" occurring (this refers to the phenomenon whereby we emotionally cut ourselves off from particular aspects of our lives, as if to protect ourselves from them). Our actions are also shaped by a traumatic reaction as well—for example, in terms of issues arising in relation to a lack of competence in the use of machinery when we are seriously distracted by the significant demands of dealing with trauma.

However, even this does not go far enough, insofar as trauma can also have biological consequences in terms of exacerbating existing health problems or creating new ones (headaches, stomachaches and so on). Furthermore, there is also the social dimension to consider for, as I empasized earlier, it is important to recognize that trauma has significant social implications. Trauma is part of the broader social sphere as well as part of an individual's personal circumstances. It would therefore be wise to consider trauma and its effects as a bio-psychosocial phenomenon—that is, one that has biological, psychological and social dimensions.

People's reactions to trauma do not follow a standard, "one size fits all" pattern. The reactions of the individual concerned will be influenced by a number of factors. These include:

- *The nature of the incident(s).* An important distinction is drawn in the literature between simple and complex trauma. A simple trauma is one that occurs on a one-off basis, a single event (note, though, that "simple" should not be equated with "easy"—even a "simple" trauma can do unspeakable harm). A complex trauma, by contrast, is one that can have much more profound and far-reaching consequences over time because the trauma is one that is repeated. Child abuse is a telling example of this [17].
- *The reactions of significant others.* How other people react, particularly those people close to us whose opinions we value, will play a part in how we react when we are subject to a trauma situation. For example, whether somebody is supportive or unsupportive, whether they reinforce a particular image of the situation we may have in our mind or not—all these factors can be very significant in influencing how we react.
- *Cultural factors.* No one exists in a cultural vacuum. We will all be influenced to a large extent by the culture we were brought up in, the culture we now live in (if different) and, to a certain extent, the culture of our workplace. Cultural influences will shape how we make sense of the situations we encounter and how we respond to them— both very important sets of factors when it comes to trauma.
- *Structural factors.* As indicated earlier in this chapter, a person's social location—that is, where he or she fits into the wider social picture—will also be significant in shaping our trauma response.
- *Other events/incidents around the time.* When we experience a trauma, other aspects of our lives do not stop functioning. The world carries on around us, and this can help or hinder, depending on what happens. We may, for example, experience other misfortunes at around about the same time we undergo a trauma which can add to our pressures (an accumulation of difficulties) or, conversely, things may coincidentally go our way at about the time a trauma occurs, and this can ease some of the pressure on us (serendipity).

An important effect of trauma is what is known as "flashbacks." This refers to experiences in which we have a brief memory of what occurred during the traumatic incident. This can be very distressing and unsettling and can severely hamper a person's recovery from what has occurred and from the damage done. This can lead to avoidance of certain places or situations or activities that may lead to a recurrence of such a memory. For example, someone who almost died through being crushed in a crowd situation may have intrusive memories of the situation which lead to him or her avoiding situations where there are there people around that may result in crowding.

Trauma involves loss and therefore initiates a grief reaction. Anger and guilt, as we shall note in Chapter 5, are common reactions to a loss. Therefore, people who have been traumatized may feel angry (directing their intense feelings outwards) or guilty (directing those feelings inwards). Of course, it is important to recognize that *feeling* guilty and *being* guilty are two very different things. Feelings of (undeserved) guilt are not uncommon in situations where people are grieving or traumatized.

A further impact is on a person's religious faith. Trauma has the effect of polarizing the situations, in the sense that a traumatic experience can have the effect of either deepening a person's religious faith or leading to him or her losing that faith.

Another common effect of trauma is a tendency to alternate between wanting to be alone—that is, valuing isolation—and clinging, attaching oneself quite closely to one or more other people. This links well with Stroebe and Schut's [18] dual process theory of grief as discussed in Chapter 1. It shows how unsettling trauma can be and how it can leave people very unsure of themselves.

Trauma also has the effect on many occasions of leading to people being what Ziegler [19] refers to as being "stuck in survival mode." This means that they can react quite strongly to anything that they see as being a potentially threatening situation, insofar as they have not managed to move beyond having feelings of being under threat. Ziegler also points out that trauma can lead to individuals pushing other people away, of reinforcing the sense of distance that can occur at such times.

Although the effects of trauma are many and varied, and can be extremely harmful, what we should not lose sight of is that these factors can interact and make each other worse. It is very easy for a vicious circle to develop. For example, a trauma can lead to somebody experiencing depression. This, in turn, can lead to that person drinking excessively. That in itself can cause further problems, such as difficulties in sleeping, problems relating to eating, and so on. Such difficulties can in turn lead to relationship difficulties and from that, opportunities for support can be cut off. Similarly, because of relationship difficulties, the tension release afforded by sexual activity may be something that becomes unavailable at a time when it could be helpful. All these difficulties can then reinforce the negative feelings that have led to the trauma-related depression.

DEALING WITH TRAUMA

Understanding trauma is an important issue in itself, but what is more important is the ability to use that understanding as a way of dealing with trauma in a helpful and constructive way. In order to discuss these issues, I shall divide my comments into three sections: before, during and after.

Preparing for Trauma

Herman makes the point that we are dealing with "horrible events" when we encounter a trauma situation:

> To study psychological trauma is to come face to face both with human vulnerability in the natural world and with the capacity for evil in human nature. To study psychological trauma means bearing witness to horrible events. [15, p. 7]

This means that we need to be quite robust, although that should not be interpreted as meaning "macho" or uncaring. We can never know whether or not a trauma is just round the corner, but it would be naïve and unwise in the extreme not to be aware that trauma is an ever-present possibility. It is therefore more appropriate to think about preparing for when the next trauma arises rather than simply wondering about whether a trauma will arise. It involves an acceptance of suffering as part of human existence. As Carol puts it, it is a matter of:

> Accepting that problems, pain and suffering are part of the life of a community, of being in the world, that they are not isolated events and cannot be avoided. Such an acceptance enables our communities to approach problems and use painful and difficult events to learn to grow and mature. [20, p. 14]

This also illustrates nicely the positive potential of trauma—it emphasizes the fact that such experiences provide opportunities for growth and transformation.

Perhaps one of the most important ways in which we can prepare for dealing with trauma is through having appropriate policies in place, and this will be one of the central topics of Chapter 4. Linked to this is the importance of training and development. There is much that staff and managers can learn about the nature and impact of trauma that can be helpful in terms of preparing people for when just such an event occurs in future.

These are clearly important and complex issues. The danger, however, is that organizations can be complacent and not do the preparatory work necessary—therefore putting themselves in a very weak and disadvantaged position if a trauma situation should arise.

Practice Focus 3.4

Bernice was the only woman on the company's board of directors. This presented some difficulties for her at times. While overt sexism did not feature, there were some very subtle ways in which Bernice found herself being undermined at times. One example was when she proposed introducing a policy on dealing with traumatic situations that may arise in the workplace. While no one rejected her proposal outright, the other members of the board nonetheless succeeded in devaluing her ideas to the point where she felt the need to withdraw her proposal. This meant that she had very mixed feelings when, less than two months later, there was a train crash in which one member of staff was killed and two others were injured. Although the injuries were not serious, the trauma that ensued was of significant proportions as the two staff concerned had actually witnessed their colleague being killed. The ramifications for the company were quite significant. Bernice was horrified by the unfolding of events, but also felt vindicated that her emphasis on the need for a policy to prepare for such matters had been well placed—despite the lack of support from her fellow board members.

Working through Trauma

Schiraldi [21] draws an important and interesting distinction between healing and recovery. Healing refers to initial stages where we begin to come to terms with what has happened. It is our initial step after going through the abyss of trauma. It is what we begin to do when we come out the other side. Recovery, by contrast, refers to the longer term process of putting our lives back in order and trying to move away from the harm done psychologically and socially to us.

Chapter 5 goes into more detail about how we can support people as they work through trauma but, for now, it is important to note an important distinction drawn by Tehrani [22, p. 83] when she talks about defusing and diffusing:

> The term *primary defusing* was introduced by Mitchell in 1983 [23]. More recently, it has been known simply as *defusing*. Mitchell said that he chose the word because it suggested that a dangerous or difficult situation was being rendered harmless. *Diffusing,* on the other hand, is a term suggested by Tehrani, Walpole, Berriman and Reilly [24]. The aim of diffusing is to assist in the gradual diffusion or melting away of the strong emotions and responses associated with a traumatic event. This is achieved through the creation of an environment in which the traumatised person can be heard and supported.

Trauma clearly presents major challenges for the workplace and therefore merits careful consideration and attention.

Recovering from Trauma

There are common themes of recovery that can be identified. For example, Herman [15, p. 3] discusses the following:

> Because the traumatic syndromes have basic features in common, the recovery process also follows a common pathway. The fundamental stages of recovery are establishing safety, reconstructing the trauma story, and restoring the connection between survivors and their community.

However, despite the apparent presence of such themes, we should not lose sight of the fact that people will respond to trauma in different ways—as we have noted, there is no "one size fits all" approach that will do justice to the complexities involved.

An important part of recovering from trauma is not just "getting over" what has happened. What we should be aiming for, where possible, is post-traumatic growth or what is often referred to as transformational grief, as discussed earlier. This involves not only returning to the pre-trauma situation, but actually going beyond it to make the most of the transformed situation. We shall return to this point in Chapter 5.

TRAUMA AND TERRORISM

Warren [25] develops an interesting analysis of terrorism and the war on terror in terms of how they can both be seen as a reaction to the trauma brought about by earlier conflicts and atrocities. There is a danger, then, that not only will terrorism cause trauma, but also further atrocities will be the result of traumatic reactions that call for blood. There is, then, a danger of a vicious circle developing.

In responding to the terrorist threat, it is important that we keep calm and avoid over-reactions. For example, the events of 9/11 have generated strong reactions in some quarters that can, in some respects, be described as examples of "Islamophobia," resulting in racist attacks on innocent, law-abiding Muslims who have done nothing to harm others. In this regard, Brewin makes helpful comment when he argues that:

> Numerous studies have shown that making death momentarily more salient leads to a variety of subtle reactions of which a person is likely unaware, such as increased liking for people who support ones worldview and increased hostility toward those with alternative worldviews (Solomon, Greenberg and Pyszczynski [26]). The message from this research is that, when thoughts of death are salient, the mere existence of people with different beliefs threatens our basis of psychological security. [1, p. 19]

This research highlights the challenges we face if we are to be in a strong position to respond to the terrorist challenge without falling into the trap of allowing prejudice and discrimination to flourish. Two wrongs, of course, do not make a right.

Nonetheless, we should not underestimate the impact of terrorism. As Charles-Edwards puts it, in drawing links between the events of 9/11 and the world of work:

> The World Trade Center was targeted by terrorists because it was a workplace, albeit one of a particular significance. The planes that were hijacked and flown into it were originally piloted and staffed by people at work. Many of the passengers were travelling on business. The fire fighters,

police and others who died in the rescue attempts were at work. They demonstrated so courageously what the commitment of people in this line of work can cost. The attacks were designed to create as many traumatic bereavements as possible, as well as heightening the anticipatory fear of being killed going to or being at work. What terrorism continues to bring to work is the sense that virtually anyone may be killed in the course of duty, a sense that in the past was restricted to jobs that were clearly dangerous. [27, pp. 152-153]

This shows just how much the western world has changed as a result of these specific incidents and the rise, in general, of terrorism as a political force.

In addressing these concerns, it is the case that, for the first time, the importance of leadership emerges, as the situation clearly involves a challenge of leadership—both politically and organizationally—if we are to be able to deal with the very real problems that have arisen in the current circumstances.

One of the positive "silver linings" of terrorism is how it can have the effect of bringing people together. It can develop a spirit of cooperation. As Raphael [28] so helpfully puts it, survival after disaster symbolizes the renewal and regeneration of the community and conveys a belief in the future. While terrorism is clearly something that should be eradicated as soon as possible, this does not mean that the positive potential for generating cohesion and a stronger sense of community (both within the workplace and in wider society) should not be capitalized upon.

CONCLUSION

Our discussions in this chapter should make it perfectly clear that trauma is a major phenomenon when it comes to the challenges of making the workplace a humane and productive environment in which people can flourish. Organizations need people for their success, and people need to be treated as people—that is, the problems and difficulties they encounter need to be recognized and appropriately dealt with. Trauma is such a complex and difficult topic that it presents major challenges. It is to be hoped, therefore, that this chapter has established just how important and just how challenging trauma can be.

The remaining chapters should go some way towards providing a platform on which we can build a solid, reasonable and effective response to the challenges involved. Such a response will need to pay heed to the policy context that governs the management of loss, grief and trauma in the workplace, and so it is to the subject of that policy context that we now turn.

REFERENCES

1. C. R. Brewin, *Posttraumatic Stress Disorder: Malady or Myth?*, Yale University Press, New Haven, Connecticut, 2003.
2. P. A. Resick, *Stress and Trauma*, Psychology Press, Hove, United Kingdom, 2001.

3. P. Bracken, *Trauma: Culture, Meaning and Philosophy,* Whurr Publishers, London, United Kingdom, 2002.
4. M. Nash, R. Munford and K. O'Donoghue (eds.), *Social Work Theories in Action,* Jessica Kingsley Publishers, London, 2005.
5. J. Nadeau, *Families Making Sense of Death,* Sage, Thousand Oaks, California, 1997.
6. J. Gordon, Foreword, in *Living with Grief at Work, at School, at Worship,* J. D. Davidson and K. J. Doka (eds.), Hospice Foundation of America, Brunner/Mazel, Washington, DC, 1999.
7. N. Thompson, *Stress Matters,* Pepar Publications, Birmingham, United Kingdom, 1999.
8. M. J. Friedman, PTSD Diagnosis and Treatment for Mental Health Clinicians, in *Trauma and Post-Traumatic Stress Disorder,* M. J. Scott and S. Palmer (eds.), Sage, London, United Kingdom and Thousand Oaks, California, 2000.
9. D. G. Cable and T. L. Martin, Effects of Public Tragedy on First Responders, in *Living with Grief: Coping with Public Tragedy,* M. Lattanzi-Licht and K. J. Doka (eds.), Hospice Foundation of America, Brunner/Mazel, Washington, DC, 2003.
10. A. Kellehear, *Compassionate Cities: Public Health and End-of-Life Care,* Routledge, London, United Kingdom and New York, 2005.
11. A. Ishmael, *Harassment, Bullying and Violence at Work,* The Industrial Society, London, United Kingdom, 1999.
12. P. Randall, *Adult Bullying: Perpetrators and Victims,* Routledge, London, United Kingdom, 1997.
13. N. Thompson, *Tackling Bullying and Harassment in the Workplace,* Pepar Publications, Birmingham, United Kingdom, 2000.
14. C. Doyle, *Working With Abused Children: From Theory to Practice* (3rd Edition), Palgrave Macmillan, Basingstoke, United Kingdom and New York, 2006.
15. J. L. Herman, *Trauma and Recovery: From Domestic Abuse to Political Terror,* Pandora, London, United Kingdom, 2001.
16. M. Tehan, The Compassionate Workplace: Leading with the Heart, *Illness, Crisis & Loss, 15*(3), 2007.
17. P. Tomlinson, *Therapeutic Approaches in Work with Traumatized Children and Young People: Theory and Practice,* Jessica Kingsley Publishers, London, United Kingdom, 2004.
18. M. Stroebe and H. Schut, The Dual Process Model of Coping with Grief: Rationale and Description, *Death Studies, 23*(3), 1999.
19. D. Ziegler, *Traumatic Experience and the Brain: A Handbook for Understanding and Treating Those Traumatized as Children,* Acacia Publishing, Phoenix, Arizona, 2002.
20. J. Carol (ed.), *Journeys of Courage: Remarkable Stories of the Healing Power of Community,* Veritas, Dublin, Ireland, 2004.
21. G. R. Schiraldi, *The Post-Traumatic Stress Disorder Sourcebook: A Guide to Healing, Recovery and Growth,* McGraw-Hill, London, United Kingdom and New York, 1999.
22. N. Tehrani, *Workplace Trauma: Concepts, Assessments and Interventions,* Brunner-Routledge, Hove, United Kingdom, 2004.
23. J. Mitchell and G. S. Everly, *Critical Incident Stress Debriefing: An Operations Manual for CISD, Defusing and Other Group Crisis Intervention Services* (3rd Edition), Chevron Publishing, Ellicott City, Maryland, 2001.

24. N. Tehrani, O. Walpole, J. Berriman and J. Reilly, A Special Courage: Dealing with the Paddington Rail Crash, *Occupational Medicine, 51*(2), pp. 93-99, 2001.

25. M. P. Warren, *From Trauma to Transformation,* Crown House, Carmarthen, United Kingdom, 2006.

26. S. Solomon, J. Greenberg and T. Pyszczynski, Pride and Prejudice: Fear of Death and Social Behavior, *Current Directions in Psychological Science, 9,* pp. 200-204, 2000.

27. D. Charles-Edwards, *Handling Death and Bereavement at Work,* Routledge, Abingdon, United Kingdom, 2005.

28. B. Raphael, *When Disaster Strikes: A Handbook for the Caring Professions,* Unwin Hyman, London, United Kingdom, 1990.

CHAPTER 4
The Policy Context

As we have noted earlier, loss, grief and trauma are, of course, very personal, even intimate, matters, but we should not allow this to blind us to the fact that there are also significant policy and legal issues to consider. This chapter sketches out the broad policy position regarding loss, grief and trauma in the workplace. The aim is not to provide detailed legal guidance, as this would go out of date quite quickly and is likely to vary quite considerably from state to state, country to country. Rather, it is a case of discussing policy principles and raising questions that good employers will need to address if they are to be as well prepared as they reasonably can be for rising to the various challenges of loss, grief and trauma in the workplace.

The chapter will help to identify: (i) what specific policy requirements need to be addressed in relation to loss, grief and trauma; and (ii) what amendments may be needed for existing policies (in relation to health and safety, for example).

The chapter begins with a discussion of two different cultural approaches to the law, followed by an exploration of health and safety concerns and the very important related concept of the "duty of care." This leads into a brief discussion of the employment law responsibilities organizations face, followed by a more detailed exploration of the policy imperatives that also require close attention.

However, before exploring some of those areas of employment law duty, it is important to establish what approach to the law is likely to be the most fruitful. What this boils down to is a distinction between *compliance* and *commitment*.

Turning again to the important theme of leadership, we can see that there are cultural issues here to consider, in the sense that an organization's culture will play a very significant role in shaping how legal matters are dealt with, whether positively or negatively. A good leader will be somebody who is able to shape a culture in the direction of a positive approach to the law, rather than a negative and defensive one. Let us consider two possible cultures that can relate to legal duties.

A CULTURE OF COMPLIANCE

In such a culture the focus is on not breaking the law. This is a defensive culture, insofar as its primary concern is "not getting into trouble." Failing to comply with legal responsibilities can be potentially disastrous for an organization in terms of the sanctions that can be put into place. For example, some companies have gone out of business because the fines they had to pay for breaking the law were of such a magnitude that they struggled to maintain profitability. In relation to the field of loss, grief and trauma, there is not only the matter of criminal law to consider (in the sense that failing to abide by certain legal responsibilities can be deemed a corporate crime), there is also the question of civil law to take into account, insofar as people who are grieving or traumatized who do not receive appropriate support may be in a position to claim damages and compensation through the legal system, if they can provide sufficient evidence that the negligence of the employing body contributed to their harm.

There are therefore strong motivating factors that push us in the direction of compliance with the law, and I would certainly not be arguing against the need to comply with the law. However, significant dangers arise when complying with the law becomes a narrow concern, unconnected with wider organizational objectives and strategies—including, for example, a commitment to staff care and well-being.

There is a considerable irony here, insofar as defensive approaches to legal compliance can actually increase the likelihood of the law being broken. That is, if we are concentrating on "covering our backs," then we can lose focus on the important issues. Once we lose our strategic direction in this way, then we increase the chances of matters going beyond our control and thus resulting in harmful consequences for all concerned.

Practice Focus 4.1

Peta was quite concerned when she was given the task of undertaking a health and safety risk assessment relating to each of the 23 staff in her section. She already felt overburdened and knew she would struggle to fit this work in. However, a local company had experienced major difficulties as a result of neglecting health and safety concerns and had lost out as a consequence of not taking the issues seriously enough. The board of Peta's company had therefore issued an instruction that all section heads must carry out risk assessments in relation to each staff member's duties. Peta thought that this was a defensive over-reaction but she knew she had to comply with the board's instructions. She therefore set about carrying out the assessments. However, while she was heavily involved in this additional onerous task, she failed to take an interest in what was happening in her section. What had escaped her attention was that Ravinder, an excellent worker and real asset to the company, had been hit hard by the death of his brother. Ravinder, feeling disgusted that Peta had not even acknowledged his loss, concluded that his employers did not value his contribution. He therefore applied for a job at a rival company and was quickly snapped up by them. Peta was shocked to find that becoming engrossed in the company's defensive reaction had ironically led to losing one of their best workers.

People who are grieving or traumatized are likely to resent strongly what they may see as cold, calculating legal compliance, rather than a genuine commitment to supporting staff through a very difficult period in their lives. This can affect not only the reputation of the organization, with potentially very detrimental effects in terms of not only recruitment and retention, but also the overall "branding" of the organization—that is, how it is perceived in the market place or the wider corporate world. We shall return to this point in Chapter 7.

A CULTURE OF COMMITMENT

Distinct from a culture of compliance is the sort of culture where the need to comply with the law is fully recognized, but it does not become a defensive priority. The primary focus is on making sure that staff and managers are committed to the organization. To secure such commitment, it is necessary to focus on their health and well-being, to make sure that they see the workplace as something they are committed to in a positive way. If such a culture of commitment can be developed, then the chances of the law being breached are considerably reduced. This is not to say that organizations can be lax or complacent about their legal duties, but rather that seeing their legal duties in the broader context of a strategic commitment to supporting staff care and well-being is a much more positive and effective approach to the issues concerned. What is needed, then, is a balance between, on the one hand, an understanding of legal requirements along and a commitment to making sure that these are met with and, on the other, a philosophy of making sure that the human resource is genuinely seen as the most important resource and, is therefore adequately looked after, not just in terms of physical matters, but also in relation to the psychological demands of the work—especially when those demands are made significantly worse by the existence of grief or trauma in people's lives.

The situation is parallel with the development of the diversity approach. For many years approaches to equality issues in the workplace were dealt with in a narrow and defensive way, again with the focus on "not getting into trouble" rather than on the more positive aim of promoting equality to make the workplace a more humane, satisfying and effective place [1]. The development of the diversity approach, with its emphasis on *valuing* diversity has helped to create the potential for developing positive approaches to equality issues. If workplaces do indeed value the individuals they employ, regardless of any differences among them, then there is likely to be less inequality. The problem with inequality can therefore be tackled in a positive way, parallel with the idea of a culture of commitment, rather than in a negative way, parallel with a culture of compliance. The cultural context in which legal responsibilities are addressed is therefore a very important part of the challenges that organizations face.

HEALTH, SAFETY AND THE
DUTY OF CARE

It has long been recognized that the workplace is a dangerous place in a number of ways. Recognition of the need for health and safety issues to be taken very seriously is not a new idea. There is a longstanding tradition of assessing risks to the health and safety of workers. This ranges from recognized high-risk situations, such as construction sites to relatively risk-free working environments (although, of course, no working environment is entirely risk free). However, an important point to note is that health and safety is not just a matter of assessing and managing physical risks—that is, risks to life and limb. There are also psychological risks to consider. For example, it is now well recognized that stress is an important feature of health and safety concerns [2]. The development of occupational health services over the years, combined more recently with the growth of employee assistance programs, bears testimony to the recognition that the workplace brings with it psychological risks as well as physical ones.

Given how distressing, and therefore potentially stressful and harmful, issues of loss, grief and trauma can be, the domain of health and safety is clearly one that needs to take account of such matters. As Rick, O'Regan and Kinder comment:

> Employers are increasingly concerned about the impact of traumatic inci-
> dents on employees. The fact that employers have a responsibility for the
> protection of employees' psychological health is well-established and
> enshrined in law. However, evidence for good practice on how to manage
> traumatic incidents in the workplace is less clear, leaving many employers
> with little or no guidance on what to do for the best. [3, p xiii]

This comment gets to the heart of this book in a sense, as it shows how important trauma is, but also acknowledges that employers are often left wondering what they need to do to respond for the best. Much the same can be said, of course, for responding to loss and grief issues.

Central to health and safety is what I shall refer to as a "duty of care." This is a term that refers to the duty placed on employers to make sure that their employees are not subjected to undue hazards of a physical or psychological nature. At the end of the day, the working environment should not be harmful to health, and that includes both physical and mental aspects of the health care spectrum.

Although it has been clearly recognized that psychological aspects of health and safety need to be considered, it is unfortunately the case that in many work settings, primacy is given to the physical aspects, often with little or no consideration of the wider issues of psychological health and the implications of this for employee well-being. This therefore raises an important question that responsible managers within organizations need to ask themselves, namely: how aware are staff and managers of the psychological aspects of health and safety? If the answer is "not very," then clearly there is much to be done to make them aware of the significant implications of loss, grief and trauma. As we have seen in the preceding chapters, these are extremely complex issues, and there are significant dangers in terms of failing to address what is involved. While much of a helpful nature can be done at the time such problems arise, this is less than optimal, insofar as preparation for such matters can leave an organization much better equipped to address the concerns rapidly and effectively as and when they arise. Leaving matters in abeyance until the problem occurs is very unwise and leaves individuals and organizations vulnerable to significant risks that could perhaps have been avoided or at least minimized. Later in this chapter, we shall consider matters relating to training and development. This is clearly one area for such work to be carried out if there is indeed a low level of awareness of the psychological aspects of health and safety in general and relating to loss, grief and trauma, in particular.

Given the complex and demanding nature of the challenges of loss, grief and trauma, there may well be a need for additional support from suitably qualified and experienced professionals outside the organization. Therefore, an important part of meeting the duty of care in relation to health and safety is to be aware of what resources are available locally, regionally and nationally. It is important to be aware of organizations that offer services, whether through statutory means, through voluntary sector provision or through the private sector. Without this knowledge, it would be difficult to connect individuals to what can be very helpful services and a network of support. See the organizations and websites section of the *Guide to Further Learning* at the end of the book for some indications of the range of possible supports available.

EMPLOYMENT LAW RESPONSIBILITIES

Although health and safety concerns clearly form one important set of legal responsibilities, they are not the only ones organizations need to take seriously. If employers are to be in a strong position to take a positive approach to helping their employees through a difficult period in their life (and thus safeguarding the interests and well-being, not only of those individuals, but also of the organization as a whole and all its stakeholders), there are other concerns that also need to be addressed—principally those issues arising from employment rights in relation to, for example, matters concerning compassionate leave and sickness absence. We shall consider these points in more detail below under the heading of "Policy Imperatives," but it is important at this stage to recognize that employment law is part of the loss, grief and trauma agenda and not something separate from it. For example, issues relating to trade union involvement can be very significant when it comes to dealing with staff well-being issues in general and in relation to loss, grief and trauma in particular. Indeed, given the staff support and protection concerns of the trade union movement, collaboration on these issues with union representatives can be potentially very fruitful as there is a clear convergence of interest in terms making sure that the health and well-being of employees are safeguarded and promoted.

Employment law varies from state to state and from country to country, and so it is not possible to give guidance that applies in relation to specific legal provision. However, there are several overarching themes that can help provide a foundation for an informed and effective approach to loss, grief and trauma. These are now considered as part of the broader picture of the policy challenges organizations face if they are to (i) fulfill their legal requirements; and (ii) generate as far as possible a culture of commitment rather than have to rely on compliance.

POLICY IMPERATIVES

The law is important in providing the overall backcloth to how matters are dealt with in the workplace. However, for managers and staff, there is an intervening level of policy, insofar as much of the work undertaken in responding to the challenges of loss, grief and trauma will be shaped not only by the broad picture of the legal context, but also by how that legal context has been translated into a set of policies within the organization concerned. In order to fulfill the legal requirements, it will therefore be necessary to consider the policy position of the organization concerned. Clearly, such matters will differ from organization to organization, but there will, of course, be certain themes in common, and it is to these that we now turn.

The whole question of policy is a very big one but, in an attempt to avoid being overambitious in trying to offer a comprehensive picture of this policy, I shall restrict myself to the following main areas: information; the media; family liaison; commemoration; sickness absence; terrorism; and training and development.

The Importance of Information

Grieving and trauma can create considerable confusion, not only for the people directly affected, but also for a wide range of people indirectly affected, including a network of people within the workplace. As an antidote to such confusion, it is important that relevant information is made available. This can include briefing staff over what has happened. For example, staff and managers may need to know that a colleague has experienced a major loss in his or her life so that they can be suitably supportive and make any necessary adjustments or allowances at the time. Similarly, if an event has occurred that affects the organization as a whole or one subsection of it, then the implications of this may need to be spelled out to employees. If people are left in the dark about what is happening, this can add to the anxiety, and thus increase the negative impact of the problems being experienced.

The Institute of Employment Studies in the UK has carried out research into the Royal Mail Group, the second largest employer in the country [3]. Part of this research is an examination of the role of what is referred to as SPoT meetings. SPoT stands for "support post trauma." These meetings are used to make sure that individuals affected by a traumatic experience are aware of what is happening and their likely responses. The same protocol could be used for people who are grieving. This is not the only way of making sure that the required information is made available but it is a useful starting point for considering the issues involved.

Information about what help may be available is an important part of this scenario. Lund [4, p. 204] makes an important point when he argues that:

> Perhaps the greatest difficulty for bereaved persons in receiving help from other people is asking for it. Nearly all bereaved persons will be told by their family members or friends to call them if they need help. Others will say, "Don't hesitate to call me if you need anything. I would like to help if you will let me know how I can." Unfortunately, 37 percent of the bereaved in one study reported having great difficulty in asking for help, even when it was offered. [5]

Providing information about what help can be made available can therefore be an important way of making it easier for employees to receive the assistance they may need. If the information has to be sought out actively by grieving or traumatized individuals, it is far less likely that they will place themselves in a position where they are able to avail themselves of what is on offer.

Practice Focus 4.2

Lin and Tony were devastated when their son, Liam, was killed in a motorcycle accident. What made it worse was that, less than an hour before the accident, they had had a very heated and unpleasant argument with him about his plans to give up his college course. They felt terrible that, not only had they lost their son, they had also parted on such poor terms—and were left wondering whether the argument had been a contributory factor in the accident, whether they had indirectly contributed to their own son's death. They both took time off work as they felt they could not cope for a while. When they did return to work, their experiences in their respective workplaces were very different. Lin was given information about what help could be made available if she needed it, including confidential counseling from the company's employee assistance program. Although she wasn't sure whether she would use the service, she felt pleased that her employers had taken the trouble to provide the information to help her make an informed choice. Tony, by contrast, was not given any information by his employers—no mention was made of any help that might have been available. Lin encouraged him to ask for the information, but Tony was reluctant to do so. He felt let down at a time when he needed more understanding from his employers, not less.

Liaison with the Media

In some circumstances, it will be necessary for information to be shared with the media—for example, in relation to any event that could be seen as newsworthy. This could include an explosion at a factory or other such events that will be of interest to local, regional, national or even international media. The very point at which a crisis situation arises is not the best time for making decisions about what information should be shared with the media and by whom. It is therefore important to plan ahead in terms of who will have responsibility for liaising with the media and how decisions will be made in a very short timescale about what information is made publicly available via such media.

Failing to handle the situation appropriately can not only cause additional pressures, tensions and possibly distress for grieving or traumatized employees, it can also do a lot of harm to the reputation of the organization concerned— especially if it becomes portrayed as uncaring, ill-equipped to deal with human issues and/or chaotic in its response. The results of being poorly prepared for liaison with the media can therefore be doubly harmful

If an organization already has a policy on media liaison, then additional consideration may need to be given to the specific demands of such communication in circumstances that involve trauma, loss of life or related matters. As we have seen, these are complex and demanding issues, and so "going live" in terms of liaison with the media without having had the opportunity to think the issues through carefully and thoroughly is leaving a great deal to chance. A well-informed, well-prepared approach is clearly a much safer bet and a far wiser strategy.

Where an organization has no policy relating to media liaison, then there is much to be gained from one. For many organizations, such a policy may never be called upon, as nothing newsworthy may occur. However, a parallel can be drawn here with fire precautions. Many organizations will never have to make use of a fire extinguisher, but they would be very unwise indeed not to have such extinguishers available.

Family Liaison

In some circumstances, there will be the necessity for a family liaison role. For example, if an individual is killed in the workplace, then a good employer would wish to be supportive of the family. This is not only a humanitarian matter, but is also important in terms of the message it gives to other employees about how they are valued. This is part of the culture of commitment referred to earlier. Consideration will therefore need to be given to who is the best person to fulfill that role, and whether he or she will need any special training in that regard. It will also be important to consider what other circumstances may necessitate the need for a family liaison—for example, as in the case of an employee who contracts a terminal illness.

In some organizations the employee assistance program (EAP) may be called upon to provide such liaison services, and that can be very effective. However, in some circumstances, the family may regard that as a sign that the organization is distancing itself from the situation. It is therefore important to ensure that such circumstances, when they arise, are handled sensitively in accordance with the specific situation rather than in a blanket fashion.

Again the question of policy arises. Are family liaison matters covered by an existing policy? If so, is such a policy sufficiently sensitive to grief and trauma issues? If not, should a specific policy be developed to cover the eventualities of a need at some point for family liaison to take place?

Commemoration

In the aftermath of a death, consideration will need to be given to whether the organization will have a role in any memorial service or contribute to, or attend, funerals. It is, of course, important to have a consistent policy on such matters so that there is no perception of unfairness if responses are carried out on an ad hoc basis. Consideration should also be given to whether there will be any form of commemoration within the organizational setting itself. For example, if a member of staff dies, will there be any form of memorial service or other way of marking the passing—perhaps a plaque, a bench in the grounds or the planting of a tree? If so, who will be involved in any such process? Who will take responsibility for making sure the process is managed effectively and sensitively?

These issues may be addressed as part of a staff care or workplace well-being policy (or equivalent) or may form the basis of a policy in its own right. Alternately, it could possibly be combined with media liaison as part of a policy on external liaison or indeed a policy specifically geared towards dealing with loss, grief and trauma issues in the workplace.

Collective rituals can also be seen as an important part of commemoration. Doka explains their significance in responding to loss:

> When organizations have experienced the death of a member or members, there is a great value in a collective ritual. This ritual, in addition to any family rituals, acknowledges the role of the lost member or members within that organization. Beyond recognizing the loss in the setting, it gives the member both unique opportunity and permission to grieve. It reaffirms the care and sensitivity of management and administration. Even in public tragedies where the organization is not directly affected, such rituals offer opportunities to

educate about grief and trauma, frame a definition of the event, and offer collective action. [6, p. 183]

This important passage highlights the very valuable role of rituals, including funerals and commemoration services, and reinforces the important message that organizations need to give careful consideration to such matters. The significance of ritual is a topic to which we shall return in Chapter 6.

Absence Arrangements

When someone experiences a significant loss or a trauma, it is likely that he or she will require some time off work. Clarity about absence arrangements therefore needs to be established. This incorporates compassionate leave and sickness absence management arrangements. Depending on the legal system in which a particular organization is operating, there are likely to be established statutory minima in terms of allowances for compassionate leave in the event of a bereavement or other traumatic event. However, whether the organization limits the allowance of compassionate leave to the statutory minimum or has a more generous policy is a matter that needs to be determined carefully in advance. Similarly, where there are sickness absence management policies in place, it will be important to ensure that these take into consideration the special circumstances that can arise in relation to loss, grief and trauma.

On a related subject, consideration may also need to be given to the possible question of suspension from duties. On very rare occasions, there may be individuals who have been so badly affected by an event in their life that it has the result of lowering their performance level to such an extent that their work is no longer of a satisfactory standard—or may even be dangerous. In such circumstances, it may be necessary to consider suspending that member of staff if he or she is not willing to take the necessary steps to address the situation (for example, if they misguidedly insist that they are "all right"). Clearly, such situations need to be handled very sensitively, but it is important not to lose sight of the fact that being compassionate and supportive is no justification for allowing dangerous practice to take place.

Hooyman and Kramer help us to understand the importance of flexibility and understanding in absence arrangements when they argue that:

Every society has rules for or norms of grieving that attempt to specify who, when, where, how, how long, and for whom people should grieve. These grieving rules are often codified in personnel policies regarding bereavement leave. For example, someone experiencing a loss that is not publicly or legally recognized, such as a young man whose partner has died of AIDS, generally cannot use bereavement leave to attend any rituals or to begin to work through his grief. [7, p. 9]

This passage clearly illustrates that a blanket approach is likely to disadvantage some people quite considerably, and so an enlightened approach that takes account of the complexities of the situation is very much to be recommended. In a similar vein, Lattanzi-Licht makes a an important point when she states that:

> Family leave time is the first rung on the ladder of corporate responsibility. Most corporate policies allow for three days of paid leave at the time of an immediate family member's death. There are few situations in which three days would be sufficient to deal with the emotional and physical realities surrounding the death of an important loved one. For family members who live across the country, travel would consume a great deal of the allotted leave time. For employees who feel punished by the loss and who experience a sense of victimization, bereavement leave policies represent limited support. Employees typically use additional days from vacation time, or take time off without pay. [8, pp. 22–23]

Some people may argue that organizations cannot afford to be more generous as they have operational concerns to address insofar as the organization's business has to continue. However, there is also a compelling argument that failing to be sufficiently compassionate and supportive will prove to be much more expensive in the long run in terms of the ill feeling and resentment that can be generated not only among those directly affected, but also among the wider staff group who witness what they see as an uncaring approach. The damage to the organization's reputation can be severe, as can the harm to any attempts to promote a culture of commitment, as discussed previously. Theses are important points to which we shall return in Chapter 7.

Practice Focus 4.3

Lin and Tony had been disappointed in how Tony's employers had responded to the death of their son in a motorcycle accident (see Practice Focus 4.2). There was further disappointment when, two months later, they had to cancel a planned vacation. After Liam's death they had both taken five days off. They were allowed three days' compassionate leave from their respective employers and had to take two days from their general leave allowance. This meant that they did not have enough leave left for their planned week's vacation in the mountains. For Lin this was no problem, as her employers indicated that they were happy to be flexible and give her the opportunity either to bring forward two days from the following year's allowance or to make up the time by working late from time to time when called upon to do so. She was pleased that they were prepared to be so flexible and it gave a clear message that she was a valued employee. For Tony, however, the situation was the reverse. His employers would not give him any flexibility at all and simply said that, if they gave him that degree of flexibility, they would have to give it to everybody and that would make the situation unworkable. The message this gave him was that he was not valued as an employee and that he had the misfortune to work for an uncaring company. It was at this point that he decided to start looking for a new job.

Terrorism

One of the reasons terror is used as a tactic by unscrupulous people pursuing a particular political agenda is that it creates great uncertainty and insecurity. The element of unpredictability creates fear and dread that, unfortunately, fits with what the terrorists are trying to achieve. Such unpredictability also makes it difficult to plan for responding to occurrences of this nature. However, there are steps that can be taken in terms of planning how to respond to a terrorism-linked event (whether a direct attack on the organization concerned, the effects of an attack elsewhere or a false alarm which nonetheless generates anxiety and distress). Increasingly organizations are including terrorism response plans in their overall business planning and policy development. Such plans are likely to be an extension of general emergency response plans and will in all probability include:

- Evacuation plans;
- Contingency plans in relation to business needs—initial crisis responses, including "psychological first aid";
- Communication arrangements; and
- Mid- to long-term responses—for example, the setting up of support groups.

Training and Development

Kirby casts important light on training and development and the role of policies when he argues that:

> Grief and traumatic grief in the workplace are significant issues that must be addressed by management. Management courses do not teach about grief, so it may be difficult for some managers to find a balance between organizational productivity and caring for the emotional well-being of employees. A company with established policies concerning grief may actually experience enhanced productivity over time. Sunoo and Solomon [9] report that 88 percent of the managers they surveyed indicated that they or a colleague recently faced, or anticipated facing, the loss of a loved one. [10, p. 42]

As Kirby implies, conventional training programs leave little if any room for loss, grief and trauma. If the policies that underpin our efforts to respond appropriately to the challenges of grief and trauma are to work, then they need to be accompanied by a strong commitment to learning and development. Attempting to provide the support needed without having had the preparation that training can provide places an organization at a disadvantage compared with organizations that have invested in exploring the insights and under-standings needed to provide a supportive workplace that makes a positive contribution to well-being and thus to personal as well as organizational effectiveness.

Consequently we can see that there is a strong need for issues relating to training and development to be given very serious consideration. Who needs to be trained in what and when? are important questions to attempt to answer. For instance, there may be a training need for senior managers in terms of developing appropriate policy responses, as outlined in this chapter. There may be general training needs relating to the overall area of dealing with the sensitive issues involved—a process of awareness raising, for example. However, there may also be specific training needs for certain individuals—for example, those providing briefing for staff members, people involved in liaison with the media, or occupying a family liaison role.

In relation to trauma issues, there will also be further training needs to consider, not least tackling bullying and harassment and handling aggression and violence which, as we noted in Chapter 3, can be significant causes of trauma. Overall, then, it should be clear that loss, grief and trauma concerns should feature in training and development plans.

* * *

This is not an exhaustive list of policy areas, but should be sufficient to paint a picture of some of the very important issues that need to be addressed in terms of policy development. They raise the question of what policy questions need to be addressed. Organizations would therefore be well advised to review their current policies and consider to what extent the concerns identified here are dealt with satisfactorily. One important aspect of such a review would be to explore whether there is a need for a stand-alone policy specifically geared towards loss, grief and trauma issues, or whether, in the organization concerned, these matters are best integrated into existing policies. For example, if there is already a policy relating to staff well-being, then it may make more sense to develop this further to incorporate loss, grief and trauma concerns, rather than start from scratch with a brand new additional policy. Whichever approach is taken, it is clearly very important indeed that these policy issues are given full consideration, so that there are no significant gaps in the provision that may cause major problems when a loss or trauma situation manifests itself at some point in the future.

Practice Focus 4.4

When Rafael was invited to become a member of his local emergency planning group, he did not appreciate what a difference it would make. He simply regarded it as one more chore to add to his list as a busy human resources manager. However, he was amazed to find out how significant the committee discussions were. He had never given a moment's thought to how his company might respond to a disaster or other public emergency, but soon became aware of the wide range of important issues involved. Significantly, it made him think about how ill-equipped his company was for any sort of unexpected event that could lead to grief or trauma—whether a public disaster or an individual tragedy. Each committee meeting made him more and more aware of what he now came to see as complacency in preparing for such eventualities. He therefore began to give a lot of thought to what changes would need to be made and what would need to be put in place to remedy the situation. He therefore decided to make an appointment to see the head of human resources in order to try and get some official backing for developing the company's policies and practices in relation to loss, grief and trauma.

CONCLUSION

In terms of the policy context, then, what it boils down to is the challenge of creating a caring and supportive work environment. As Carol puts it:

> After the tragic events of September 11, 2001, those of us who lived in New York City soon realized how critical it was to be a part of a community, to join forces with others in order to lick our wounds, to grieve our losses, and to begin the process of recovery and healing. Without much thought or planning, we somehow were galvanized to pull together and reach out to each other in our suffering and need. I'm certain the process of our "healing" from the horror of that day was enhanced because of a sense of fellowship—not only with each other in New York City but with people throughout the world who felt like an extension of our community too. An extraordinary, cooperative spirit emerged from this tragedy. [11, pp. 10–11]

These issues will be addressed more fully in Chapter 5 where the emphasis is on providing care and support and will also feature in Chapter 7. However, for present purposes, it is important to note that the workplace is an important site for responding to loss and trauma—it is part of the community to which Carol refers. Workplace communities develop in their own way in their own time, partly as a result of the personalities involved and the interactions between them. However, leadership is also an important part of shaping and developing workplace communities. Having appropriate, well-informed policies, combined with a culture of commitment, will be vitally important as a foundation for developing such a caring and effective community of colleagues.

Policy issues can be addressed in a purely administrative, almost mechanistic, way to make sure that the t's are crossed and the i's are dotted. However, in dealing with such complex and challenging subject matter as loss, grief and trauma, such an approach is likely to be far from adequate. What is needed, then, is not so much a bureaucratic or administrative approach to these issues, but rather one that is based on leadership—that is, on the skills involved in being able to create a culture of commitment in which employees feel valued and supported and are therefore prepared to pull together at times of need in order to make sure that people are operating in a humane and competent workplace.

Hooyman et al. make a significant point when they comment that:

> Individuals faced with loss need social and economic supports to give them time and opportunity to grieve fully. The positive effects of social support on physical and mental health have been extensively documented [12]. Similarly, a perception of positive social support is usually identified with a positive adaptation to loss [13, 14]. Social support may consist of family, friends, neighbors, acquaintances, and others in the larger community. [7, p. 81]

The workplace is clearly an important part of that larger community and therefore shares some degree of responsibility for providing support. Getting the policy context right is a major part of trying to make such a supportive community a reality.

REFERENCES

1. N. Thompson, *Promoting Equality: Tackling Discrimination and Oppression,* Palgrave Macmillan, Basingstoke, United Kingdom and New York, 2003.
2. M. Schabracq, C. Cooper, C. Travers and D. van Maanen, *Occupational Health Psychology: The Challenge of Workplace Stress,* British Psychological Society, Leciester, United Kingdom, 2001.
3. J. Rick, S. O'Regan and A. Kinder, *Early Intervention Following Trauma: A Controlled Longitudinal Study at Royal Mail Group,* Institute for Employment Studies, Brighton, United Kingdom, 2006.
4. D. A. Lund, Giving and Receiving Help During Later Life Spousal Bereavement, in *Living with Grief at Work, at School, at Worship,* J. D. Davidson and K. Doka (eds.), Hospice Foundation of America, Brunner/Mazel, Washington, DC, 1999.
5. I. S. Rigdon, *Toward a Theory of Helpfulness for the Elderly Bereaved: An Invitation to a New Life,* unpublished doctoral dissertation, University of Utah College of Nursing, 1985.
6. K. J. Doka, Memorialization, Ritual, and Public Tragedy, in *Living with Grief: Coping with Public Tragedy,* M. Lattanzi-Licht and K. J. Doka (eds.), Hospice Foundation of America, Brunner-Routledge, Washington, DC, 2003.
7. N. R. Hooyman and B. J. Kramer, *Living Through Loss: Interventions Across the Life Span,* Columbia University Press, Chichester, United Kingdom, 2006.
8. M. Lattanzi-Licht, Grief in the Workplace: Supporting the Grieving Employee, in *Living with Grief at Work, at School, at Worship,* J. D. Davidson and K. J. Doka (eds.), Hospice Foundation of America, Brunner/Mazel, Washington, DC, 1999.

9. B. P. Sunoo and C. M. Solomon, Facing Grief: How and Why to Help People Heal, *Personnel Journal, 75*(4), pp. 78-89, 1996.
10. M. Kirby, Grief in the Law Enforcement Workplace: The Police Experience, in *Living with Grief at Work, at School, at Worship,* J. D. Davidson and K. J. Doka (eds.), Hospice Foundation of America, Brunner/Mazel, Washington, DC, 1999.
11. J. Carol, *Journeys of Courage: Remarkable Stories of the Healing Power of Community,* Veritas, Dublin, Ireland, 2004.
12. M. S. Stroebe and H. Schut, Models of Coping with Bereavement: A Review, in *Handbook of Bereavement Research,* M. S. Stroebe, R. O. Hansson, W. Stroebe and H. Schut (eds.), American Psychological Association, Washington, DC, 2001.
13. T. A. Rando, *Treatment of Complicated Mourning,* Research Press, Champaign, Illinois, 1993.
14. X. S. Ren, K. Skinner, A. Lee and L. Kazis, Social Support, Social Selection and Self-Assessed Health Status: Results from the Veterans' Health Study in the United States, *Social Science and Medicine, 12,* pp. 1721-1734, 1999.

CHAPTER 5
Providing Care and Support

Supporting people who are grieving or traumatized can be stressful work for managers and colleagues and can "open up old wounds." It is therefore important to consider the support needs of not only staff directly affected by grief or trauma, but also caregivers who can find providing care and support at such difficult times to be a potentially stressful undertaking. This chapter provides helpful guidance on the issues to consider and the steps that need to be taken.

We begin by revisiting the theme of staff care and workplace well-being, as initially discussed in Chapter 1, and reaffirming its importance as a foundation for rising to the challenges of loss, grief and trauma. This leads into a discussion of what is usually referred to as "normal" grieving (although, as we shall see, the idea of normality can be misleading). Next comes a discussion of "complicated" grieving—that is, those forms of grieving that are considered to be problematic in some way. Responding to trauma is also explored as an important part of providing care and support. Finally, we ask the vitally important question: How can we help?

STAFF CARE AND WORKPLACE
WELL-BEING

There is a saying in the retail world that if you do not look after your customers, somebody else will. That is, if you do not have the appropriate level of customer care, then you will lose customers to your competitors. Much the same can be said of staff care, in the sense that, if an organization does not look after its staff, then, at best, they will lose them. At best? Yes, because what is worse than losing staff is keeping staff who are demotivated, disaffected and potentially a liability to the organization concerned, especially as their negativity can undermine the efforts and commitment of other employees who may become "infected" by the low morale of some of their colleagues. There are very strong ethical and humanitarian reasons why employing organizations should have an ethos of staff care and a commitment to workplace well-being, but also beyond that, there is very sound business sense that tells us that, if people are indeed our most important resource, then it would be very foolish indeed not to make sure that their needs are met and that they are adequately supported and valued for the contributions that they make.

Kahan [1] introduced an important topic when she wrote of "the competent workplace." By this what she meant is the sort of workplace that employs managers who have the skills to make sure that staff are indeed adequately supported and valued. This is an important term when we consider the challenges of loss, grief and trauma. What is needed, then, is the development and maintenance of the necessary wherewithal for sustaining a competent workplace. This raises a number of important questions to consider:

- Do you use an employee assistance program (EAP)? If so, does it offer more than counseling? Consider, for example, the possibility of drawing on occupational social work services [2]. There are dangers in terms of seeing counseling as being a panacea for all problems that have any sort of emotional dimension to them. We shall return to this point later under the heading of "How can we help?" (page 92)
- Are your occupational health services tuned in to loss, grief and trauma issues? Do they understand the sensitivities and subtleties involved? Have the staff had appropriate training on such matters, or are they relying on their general professional education?
- Are managers and human resources staff aware of the situation concerning loss, grief and trauma? In particular, are they aware of the dangers of "medicalization"? (We shall discuss this in more detail below.)

An important part of an ethos of staff care is being able to balance negatives and positives. Clearly when we are talking of grief and trauma, we are referring to situations characterized by considerable pain and suffering. There are inevitably negatives involved in this. However, referring back to the notions of post-traumatic growth and transformational grief discussed earlier in the book, we should not lose sight of the potential for promoting growth and transformation, or drawing out the positives of the situation as well as recognizing and addressing the negatives involved. This is no easy challenge and brings us back to the important topic of leadership. Good leaders will be well tuned in to these concerns and will be in a strong position to shape a culture that is sensitive to the negatives, but does not fail to recognize the positives in terms of promoting growth and development at such times. This is a highly skilled undertaking, but one that is not beyond the means of a good leader.

TYPICAL GRIEVING

When we experience a major loss, the very foundations of our being can be shaken. We can lose what is referred to in the textbooks as "ontological security" [3]. This can mean that people who are grieving feel that they are going mad; that they are losing their grip on reality, because their everyday, taken-for-granted assumptions no longer seem to apply. It is therefore important to establish that this is quite a common feature of a grief reaction, and should therefore not be seen as in any way a sign of mental disorder.

It is also important not to confuse grieving with another mental disorder, namely depression. The work of Schneider on this subject has shown how dangerous it can be to fail to appreciate the significant differences between the two [4].

Fitzgerald [5] describes grief as a "rollercoaster" experience. She goes on to make the important point that this too is "normal," in the sense of being quite typical or common. Indeed, dual process theory, as discussed in Chapter 2, will help us to understand that this is par for the course in terms of the trajectory that grieving usually follows, that it will not be a smooth movement from one stage to the next, but rather an oscillation between a focus on the past and all that is now lost from that past, and the future and how that needs to be rebuilt [6].

People who are grieving will experience a wide range of emotions. This will range from sadness or extreme sorrow through to anger and bitterness at the other extreme. All these emotions are generally underpinned by a profound sense of emptiness. There is no "correct" set of emotions, although some emotional responses may lead to further problems (for example, an angry response may lead to an escalation of tensions that could spill over into aggression or even violence). Such emotions are not only wide ranging, but also quite intense—something that can lead many people to back away, as they are likely to find such intensity of emotion quite unsettling and very uncomfortable. This can mean that people who are grieving can sometimes be left without the support they need, as people who would otherwise be supportive have been prevented from helping by their own emotional response.

Another important aspect of common or typical patterns of grieving is what is referred to as survivor guilt [7]. This describes the strong sense of guilt that people can experience when somebody close to them has died or when they have been alongside somebody that they may not have known very well who dies—for example, in a transport accident such as a bus crash. Feelings of guilt are quite common when people are grieving, and so this guilt can be rationalized in terms of having a sense that "it should have been me," rather than the person who did actually die. Again, while this may seem quite bizarre, verging on madness, it is in fact a fairly typical part of grieving.

Practice Focus 5.1

Brad noticed that his next-door neighbor, Lee, was struggling to get his car started. Although not a qualified mechanic, Brad knew a lot about cars, and so he went over to help Lee with his problem. It turned out to be a relatively straightforward fault to fix and Lee was soon on his way, very grateful to Brad for his help. However, what was to happen later that day was not so positive. On the way to work Lee was involved in an accident in which he was seriously injured. He died later that day in hospital. When Brad found out what had happened, he was wracked with guilt. He felt that he was indirectly responsible for Lee's death. If only he had not helped him fix his car, Lee would still be alive. Lee's death was down to him—these were the thoughts that kept coming back into his mind. He couldn't stop thinking about how his "interference" had led to such tragic consequences. His wife, Gina, tried to reassure him that he was only doing his neighbor a favor and could not be held responsible for what happened to Lee. However, what Gina was saying was very logical and sensible, but what Brad was experiencing was not a rational reaction. It was a very intense emotional grief reaction. He could not explain it rationally, but the feelings of guilt would not go away. It was to be some months before Brad was able to think more rationally about what had happened. He still felt bad about it, but slowly came round to recognizing that he was not responsible.

"COMPLICATED" GRIEVING

For many years, what we now refer to as complicated grieving went under the heading of "pathological" grieving. This implied that there was something wrong with an individual who was grieving in what could be described as a non-standard way. We now tend to adopt a less judgmental approach to these issues by recognizing that grief is not a simple matter of one size fits all. Different people will grieve in different ways and, before attaching a negative label to somebody's grieving process, we should think very carefully about the implications.

Complicated grief therefore refers to those situations where an individual may be experiencing difficulties (or causing difficulties for others) by grieving in ways that are different from how others generally grieve. For example, complicated grief can manifest itself as delayed or extended grief. In the former case, concern can arise because an individual does not seem to be showing any signs of going through a grief reaction. It is as if they have been frozen in trauma and are not able to move on with their lives. In the latter case, it is as if no resolution to grief can be found and the pain and suffering associated with grief are continuing to predominate in a person's life. Such complications can arise because of the factors identified in Chapter 2, namely multiple, cumulative or unexpected losses. Similarly, disenfranchised losses—through suicide, for example—can have a complicating effect.

What is leading to the grief being problematic in some way can sometimes be very apparent, but in many cases, there are very complex factors at work that may not be visible to the individual concerned or those trying to help. For example, there may be significant issues in the individual's previous experiences of grieving that are leading to complications. Or it may be that how one or more other people are reacting to this loss that is at the root of it. Additionally, there may be factors in the relationship that complicate matters—for example, if the person grieving had fallen out with the deceased but had not had the opportunity for a reconciliation before death intervened.

The term "complicated grief" is a very appropriate one, insofar as these are very clearly complicated issues. For example, what counts as problematic grieving will differ from culture to culture. Rosenblatt [8, p. 41] gives a good example of this:

> One may think of grief as a human universal and grief pathologies as also universal, but the reality is that grief is quite different from culture to culture. So what, if anything is considered a grief pathology differs widely from culture to culture. A mother in the slums of Cairo, Egypt, locked for seven years in the depths of a deep depression over the death of a child is not behaving pathologically by the standards of her community [9]. A bereaved Balinese who seemingly laughs off a death is also behaving appropriately by the standards of her culture [10]. Similarly, in another society a person who is possessed by the spirits of the dead may be in line with what is entirely understandable and quite common in bereavement in her own society.

There will also be gender differences in terms of how people are likely to go through a grief reaction. For example, the work of Martin and Doka [11] has shown that there are two distinct styles of grieving, and that most men prefer an "instrumental" style, while most women appear to prefer an "affective" style.

Complicated grief should not be confused with intense grief. Describing a grief reaction as complicated is not the same as commenting on how intensely or strongly a grief reaction is felt. The term "complicated" is used when there seems to be some sort of problem or failure of recovery in terms of grieving. In some respects, this is parallel with the notion of post-traumatic stress disorder (PTSD), PTSD is not a "normal" reaction to a trauma, but rather a more serious situation where the individual concerned does not appear to be recovering from the traumatic reaction over time. He or she appears to be stuck in a difficult phase. Complicated grief is parallel with this, in the sense that it is not a matter of the nature or intensity of the reaction but the fact that, in some way, it seems that the individual is not grieving in a way that is allowing him or her to move forward.

For many years much of the literature relating to loss and grief was based on the idea that there is a "correct" or healthy way to grieve and that anyone who deviated from this was experiencing abnormal or pathological grief. We now have a much more sophisticated understanding of the complex and variable nature of grief reactions, and we are much more fully aware of the dangers of responding inappropriately to someone who is grieving a significant loss. We now know that how we help needs to be based on a careful assessment of the situation and that we cannot work on the basis of a standardized model of what counts as healthy grieving.

This means that we cannot simply assume that someone who is not grieving as we might expect is having problems in grieving. However, this does not mean that there are no problematic forms of grieving. There will be a wide range of approaches to grief that will work for the individual concerned and we must not make the mistake of equating that diversity of responses with a deviation from a "healthy" norm or "correct" way of grieving. However, there will also be some approaches to grieving that do not work, in the sense that they cause problems for the individual concerned and/or possibly for other people. Possible complicated grief examples would include:

- *Trying not to grieve.* This can involve simply trying to block out any thoughts or feelings about the loss. This can lead to dissociation, a numbing of the feelings that can distort our perceptions of reality and lead to tensions with others.
- *Not making adjustments.* Loss brings about a significant transition in our lives. Some people can find it extremely difficult to make the transition and may not make the adjustments necessary. In some respects this is an exaggeration of common patterns of grieving. For example, a woman who has lost her husband may continue to set a place at the table for him for some considerable time after his death—it can become a ritual. However, we would not tend to regard this as complicated grieving, whereas a situation in which someone tries to live their life as if the loss has not occurred may well result in the term "complicated grief" being applied—perhaps in circumstances where a woman whose husband, the sole breadwinner in the family, has died, but she makes no effort—over a period of months—to arrange an alternative source of income. It is as if she has become stuck or even paralyzed in her grief.
- *Mental health problems.* In some cases a major loss can lead to mental health problems, such as severe depression, or can exacerbate pre-existing conditions.
- *Drug and alcohol problems.* Grief can lead some people to overindulge in alcohol or to misuse drugs (illegal drugs or prescription medication), and the problems this brings are then likely to lead to difficulties in dealing with the significant challenges a major loss brings.
- *Causing problems for others.* Some people's grief reactions can involve being aggressive or vindictive towards others. This can lead to a vicious circle in which other people's reactions to being treated badly can raise tensions and add to the distress.

RESPONDING TO TRAUMA

Trauma and loss are very closely linked, in the sense that trauma can lead to losses and certain losses can, in themselves, be traumatic. However, it would be a mistake to confuse loss and trauma. This is because traumatic and grief reactions follow different trajectories—that is, while they have much in common, they also have certain differences that need to be taken into consideration. For example, a primary difference is that, in most cases, grief will resolve itself over time (although it has to be recognized that we will generally never "get over" a major loss), while there is considerable evidence to suggest that traumas will not necessarily resolve themselves over time. As Rick, O'Regan and Kinder comment:

> Many people spontaneously recover from traumatic incidents. However, population estimates suggest that a significant group (typically around 25 per cent will not recover on their own and could benefit from some kind of support). There are no specific figures for recovery from traumatic incidents at work. [12, p. xii]

The importance of recognizing that traumas will often create the need for supportive interventions is especially significant in relation to children and young people. For example, the pioneering work of the UK-based child care organization SACCS (www.saccs.co.uk) has shown over 20 years that it is naïve to expect children to recover from trauma without skilled and well-informed interventions. Providing a caring and nurturing environment is a necessary condition for helping children recover from trauma, but it is not a sufficient condition [13].

Another significant difference is that loss situations will often have rituals associated with them that help to provide a sense of stability; an anchor in a storm as it were. Trauma is far less likely to be accompanied by such rituals. This can be very significant, as a traumatic reaction will often generate a strong sense of social isolation and so, if there is no social support (whether through rituals or otherwise) offered at the time, the traumatic reaction may be intensified due to the additional uncertainty and vulnerability that can be generated by the lack of social supports.

Because of this, organizations need to be very careful about how they address trauma situations to ensure that the individuals concerned are not left feeling isolated and unsupported. As Everstine and Everstine helpfully explain:

> Employees look to management for support and assistance when traumatic situations occur. A sensitive approach by management can become a major force in how swiftly and thoroughly the employees will recover. Managers who take an overly defensive, aloof or adversarial position in these matters—due often to their fear of litigation—can make the situation far worse. Sometimes, such a defensive approach will exacerbate the employee's anger and lead him or her toward acting-out or litigation, whereas a neutral, even-handed, caring approach will serve the best interests of all. Most traumatized employees can return to proper functioning if they are treated reasonably. [14, p. 281]

Practice Focus 5.2

Miriam had experienced a number of major losses and, while this didn't make any loss easier to bear, it did mean that she knew what supports she could rely on. However, when she was assaulted in the street and had her purse stolen, the incident hit her hard. She lost her confidence about going out alone; she looked at all men with suspicion (her assailant was male); and she felt her whole sense of security in the world had been destroyed. She consulted a therapist who was able to help her understand that she had been traumatized and to explore ways in which she could recover from this over time. Miriam found this helpful and was appreciative of the support she received. However, in comparing her current situation with her previous experiences of loss, what she realized was that there were no supportive rituals—no cards of condolence, no funeral or wake, no commemoration service. It was only now that she understood how important such rituals were. She regarded them as a metaphorical "holding hands"—where people came together to acknowledge and validate the loss and express a sense of solidarity in coping with the pain, suffering and deprivations involved. But, in dealing with an equally painful and difficult experience as a result of being robbed, she found she had no such sense of "we are in this together" due to the absence of rituals. It made her feel even more isolated and therefore even more vulnerable.

HOW CAN WE HELP?

Chapter 4 was concerned with the policy context and looked at how organizations need to give very careful attention to policy issues if they are to play a constructive role in addressing loss, grief and trauma in the workplace. These interventions at a policy level can therefore be described as macro-level responses to the challenges involved. Here we switch our concern to what could be called micro-level responses—looking at how, at a level of individual interactions, we can provide a helpful response to the situations that arise.

"Being There"

It may sound trite, but when somebody is grieving or traumatized, what they may need at first is simply somebody to be there for them, somebody who may not be actually doing anything (because often there is nothing that can be done), but whose presence and connection are showing concern and thus providing an important source of support. Unfortunately, one thing that can prevent this from happening is a strong tendency for people to avoid the painful situations related to grief and trauma, to cross the road, as it were, to avoid the potential embarrassment and difficulties involved in dealing with the highly sensitive issues of supporting somebody who is in a very sad place as a result of a loss or traumatic experience.

Similarly, we have to be careful not to allow the trivializing of the situation. Because of their embarrassment and feelings of uncertainty about how to speak to somebody who is grieving or traumatized, it is very common for people to come up with what can be seen as trivial comments. For example, it is not unusual for people who are perhaps genuinely trying to be supportive to have the opposite effect by making comments that play down the significance of the issue. In particular, it can be dangerous to give false reassurance. To say to somebody, for example, that "everything will be OK" when that person is feeling that, at that particular time, nothing is OK, can be unhelpful in the extreme. The danger, then, is that people can either go to one extreme of not being involved at all (that is, avoidance) or go to the other extreme of playing down the significance of the issues. There is, of course, a helpful and healthy balance in between these two extremes that involves having a degree of sensitivity and being "tuned in" to what is happening to an individual when they are grieving or undergoing a traumatic reaction.

Attig also makes the important point that we should avoid giving simple advice. This is in a sense a variation on the theme of not trivializing the matter:

> Mourners are put off by others who fail to see how the shape and proportion of what lies before them is anything but ordinary and who offer simple advice about what they need to address their losses. They rightly set aside books that give no hint of understanding how daunting their situation is, and they reject those who try to comfort them by parroting superficial words of understanding. Grieving reminds them, and us of the profundity, of the mystery of living an individual life, in which struggles with finiteness, change, uncertainty and vulnerability recur and persist. [15, p. 15]

This passage is typical of the important and sensitive insights to be found in Attig's writings [15, 16]. It is helpful in indicating the degree of sensitivity we need to develop if we are to be as effective as we can be in supporting people through experiences of loss and trauma.

Individual Interventions

The point was made earlier that EAPs can at times go beyond counseling. One of the problems associated particularly with bereavement is that there is a strong tendency for people to assume that, if somebody is grieving, the appropriate response is to offer bereavement counseling. This is mistaken on two grounds. First of all, somebody who is grieving may not need any assistance it all. It would be a serious mistake to assume that grief necessarily produces a situation that the individual cannot cope with unaided. Making such an assumption can be very disempowering. As Kellehear puts it:

> Frequently we leave death and loss to the psychological professions and in this way support the falsity that death is an individual and private matter. . . . we no longer speak about the universality of loss or the commonplace ordinariness of death, dying and loss. And except for significant disasters, we seldom recognize every individual's death and loss as a community experience . . . Recently two students were shot dead at one of the local universities in my city. I watched the television news coverage of the aftermath and was struck by a reporter's final observations in her report: "Students and staff at the university are being provided with counselling". I would like to live in a society where the first words about comfort and healing are recorded in the following way: ". . . and staff and students are now talking and commiserating with family and friends." [17, pp. viii–ix]

And, of course, we need to remember that the workplace is a significant dimension of that community. We could then perhaps add to Kellehear's very wise words as follows: ". . . commiserating with family, friends *and colleagues.*"

Second, it is a mistake to assume that counseling is the only or even the best response to situations where somebody does need help in coping with their grief. Thompson and Bevan [18] refer to the importance of what they call "bereavement interventions"—that is, moving beyond simply assuming that, whatever the problem in relation to a loss, the answer is counseling. Counseling can be extremely effective in those situations where having the opportunity to talk issues through is an appropriate and helpful response, but it is potentially dangerous to overgeneralize the role of counseling. For example, where a parent has lost a child, then there may be a great need for assistance in a wide range of factors—practical and financial, perhaps—that are of more pressing concern than any need for talking through the emotional dimension of the situation. This is where occupational social work can be a useful alternative to simply assuming that counseling is the answer [2]. Social workers at times adopt counseling as a suitable method of intervention, but will also draw on a wide repertoire of other problem-solving interventions as appropriate [19].

Both grief and trauma can play havoc with our sense of meaning. They can have the effect of turning upside down what is often referred to as our "assumptive world." That is, our whole framework of meaning can be unsettled, if not shattered, by a major loss or a trauma. In recognition of this, we have seen the development of meaning reconstruction theory [20, 21]. Central to this theoretical perspective is the importance of narrative or storytelling:

> For centuries, storytelling has been used as a powerful and beneficial tool in the healing process. Healing stories can touch our hearts and help us understand that life is a series of challenges—not all good, not all bad. Healing stories can help us expand our consciousness so that we can see our lives and the world in new ways. Yes, telling and hearing stories can be powerful medicine. [22, p. 16]

Workplace issues, as important features of an individual's identity and sense of where he or she fits into the wider world, will clearly be significant aspects of the stories that emerge at a time of loss or trauma.

Gelfand, Raspa, Briller and Schim also have important comments to make on this subject:

> Narrative gives us the power to make sense of life. It is the central instantiation of the human mind, as Jameson [23] observes. In other words, story-making is the characteristic way humans use their mental powers. This process is a way to make meaning and give coherence to the random flow of events. [24, p. 4]

While helping people to develop a new narrative that helps them address their new circumstances, in situations relating to trauma, it also has to be recognized that there may need to be a degree of repetition to support that narrative. Simply changing the narrative can be helpful up to a point but, given the nature of trauma, this may not be enough and certain patterns of behavior and belief may need to be reinforced by constant repetition over time if the approach is to be helpful in responding to trauma situations [25].

Solomon and Siegal also emphasize that it is important that we use whatever resources available to us to contradict the sense of helplessness that can characterize both trauma and grief. This involves helping people establish a degree of power and control in circumstances where they feel helpless and powerless:

> To make meaning of the traumatic experience usually is not enough. Traumatized individuals need to have experiences that directly contradict the emotional helplessness and physical paralysis that accompany traumatic experiences. [26, p. 188]

An important goal in the human services is to avoid dependency creation. This can be particularly significant in matters relating to loss and trauma, as the people so affected may be so "at sea" and confused that they become very susceptible to the influence of others and possibly become less self-reliant. It is for this reason that it is important to place emphasis on *empowerment*—helping people gain greater control of their lives [27]. This theme of promoting a greater sense of control and gently challenging feelings of helplessness and powerlessness is therefore an important principle of good practice in supporting people through experiences of loss and trauma.

Overall, we can identify three elements of the process of helping. The first involves establishing a degree of safety. When people are grieving or traumatized, they can feel very insecure. We therefore need to give careful consideration to what can be put in place to help to establish a sense of safety and security. This can range from practicalities (for example, if somebody has been assaulted, it can amount to putting in place safety measures to ensure that this person is protected from further assaults) to a situation of offering emotional support to someone who is in need of the warmth and security that contact with caring other people can generate. The second element is what was described in Chapter 3 as "healing." This involves the early stages of helping somebody come to terms with the situation they find themselves in. The third element is "recovery." In trauma situations, this involves helping people to get to the point where they can look at how they can grow as a result of the painful experiences they have undergone. It can be a positive process of putting the negativities behind us and establishing a new balance or "homeostasis" (emotional stability). However, it is important to note that, in relation to grief, the matter of recovery is not quite so simple. This is because it has to be recognized that, in terms of major losses, there cannot be a situation where we simply "recover," as if we are getting over an illness. Recovery in relation to grieving should therefore be seen as a process of helping people establish a new life that maintains the person or thing they have lost as part of that life, but in a new context. In this sense, we are looking at grief as a transition.

Practice Focus 5.3

Emma was quite devastated when she learned that her home had been entirely destroyed by a gas explosion. The authorities were very supportive of her. First, they made sure that she was safe and had somewhere to stay by helping her to make contact with her sister in another part of the city. Second, she was offered support in coming to terms with losing her home, all her treasured possessions and memories and with them her sense of security and rootedness. She was in such a state of shock that she very much valued this help and show of concern. Third, she was offered the opportunity to have longer-term support to help her rebuild her shattered life and to make the necessary adjustments that this unfortunate accident had forced upon her. She realized that the support services could not bring her home back or take away the acute pain she felt as a result of having her world turned upside down, but she nonetheless appreciated the caring help she was being offered at a time when she felt extremely vulnerable.

Schneider [4, p. 5] provides a set of questions that can help us to address these transition issues:

What is lost?
How bad is it?
What is left?
Can it be restored?
What is possible?
What new possibilities might now exist?

These can be put to good use in creating a sense of order and structure in what can otherwise be experienced as chaotic and distressing. They can provide a clear focus for discussion when the individual concerned is ready to begin rebuilding—that is, when he or she is moving from healing to recovery. They can also form a useful focus for group support (discussed below).

In addressing issues of trauma in particular, one helpful strategy can be that of desensitization. This involves exposing people bit by bit to small elements of whatever it is they have become frightened of. For example, if somebody was traumatized by being involved in a near fatal road traffic accident (or fatal for a loved one), then what may be necessary is for the individual concerned to be reintegrated into such forms of transport on a gradual basis, with full support at each stage. People who are "thrown in at the deep end" are likely to learn how to drown, rather than learn how to swim. In dealing with such matters, it is therefore important that we are careful to ensure that we take things slowly and carefully at the pace of the individual concerned. However, it is important to note that desensitization may not be enough on its own to deal with the situation. It may need to be supported by other interventions such as counseling or group support.

Grief reactions can produce, as was noted earlier, a strong sense of guilt—often very irrational guilt that has no basis in the objective facts of what has occurred. What can be very helpful, therefore, is for supportive people to assist with the transition from feelings of guilt to feelings of regret. We can subtly help people who may be stuck in a sense of guilt characterized by the notion of "if only . . ." by concentrating on issues of regret. This may seem to be simply playing with words but, in reality, it can be a very significant transition for individuals to make. It involves depersonalizing the feelings, in the sense of recognizing that emotions that may seem very like guilt are quite normal at times of grief and trauma, but they are more constructively re-clothed as experience of regret. In a way, this is a form of narrative therapy [28, 29] insofar as it involves developing a new narrative, story or thread of meaning (one of regret) to replace an unhelpful one (of guilt).

In recent years, we have seen the development of a strong emphasis on solution-focused approaches [30]. This involves not focusing on where situations are going wrong, but rather on where they are going right. For example, if somebody is depressed much of the time, rather than focusing on the depression and how this may possibly be tackled, a solution-focused approach would focus on those situations where the individual concerned does not feel depressed and looking at how these experiences can be built on and maximized. This positive focus can, in certain circumstances, be extremely effective. However, despite the strengths of this approach, we have to recognize that it has limitations in relation to trauma situations. This is because the person whose life has been turned upside down may find it extremely difficult to focus on positives. This is not to rule out the use of solution-focused approaches, but rather to be clear that we should not have unrealistic expectations of what such an approach can achieve. It also warns us that such approaches need to be used carefully and not in an uncritical spirit of enthusiasm because of their success in other areas.

Finally, in terms of individual interventions, it is important to consider the topic of debriefing. There has been considerable debate over the value of debriefing. Tehrani's comments on this matter are instructive:

> While it has been shown that the legal process can have a negative impact on the psychological well-being of victims of trauma, it is also true that the current unresolved debate on the benefits or otherwise of debriefing and trauma counselling is also unhelpful. Given the growing body of negative literature relating to trauma debriefing and counselling, organisations are uncertain whether providing debriefing as part of a post-trauma care pro-gramme will increase rather than decrease their vulnerability to litigation. [31, p. 58]

At one time debriefing was seen as unquestionably a positive form of support. However, more recently, as Tehrani indicates, some research studies have sug-gested that, in some circumstances at least, debriefing can cause distress (for example, when going over the traumatic events can have the effect of opening up the wounds). This does not mean that debriefing should never be used, but rather that it should be used with caution—making sure as far as is reasonably possible that it is being used at the right time, in the right way and with the right person—rather than as standard practice across the board as was once the case.

Where debriefing is to be used, then it can be helpful to consider its goals. Referring to the work of Everly and Mitchell [32], Warren [33] points out that the three goals of debriefing can be summarized as:

1. *Stabilization.* This involves mitigating the acute stress that an individual may be experiencing at the time.
2. The second goal is *restoration.* This involves a return to what is known as homeostasis—that is a steady state of psychological functioning or emotional stability.
3. The third goal is a *reduction* of the level of difficulty being experienced, helping people to return to their normal level of functioning.

This fits broadly with the three-element approach discussed above (see Practice Focus 5.3).

Group Support

Group support can be divided into two types. There is the formal type of support, such as group work [34]. This involves working *with* groups—usually in a structured way. The second type is informal. This comprises colleague and management support and can be characterized as support *through* groups—that is, where being a member of a supportive group provides considerable emotional sustenance. Both kinds of support are very important when it comes to tackling these matters.

The significant role of group support is confirmed by the fact that individuals do not exist in isolation, they are part of a social network, or what Hedtke and Winslade [35, p. 7] refer to as a "club":

> A person's membership club serves as a major reference point for the construction of identity. In the relationships between a person and the other members of the club of his or her life, identity positions are offered and taken up and identifications are authenticated. From this perspective, identity is a by-product of multitudes of dialogues with others around us who validate us to be who we are [36].

Similarly, Neimeyer makes an important point about the significance of connectedness and this is something that very clearly applies to the workplace:

> All too often, mourning is described as if it were a strictly individual process, as if each of us were an island buffeted by the waves of misfortune, unconnected to anyone or anything beyond ourselves. While loss does indeed have deeply personal meanings, and we must respect our need to do some of our "grief work" privately, it is worth reminding ourselves that much of this grief work has to do with affirming, strengthening, and enlarging our connectedness to others. [37, p. 53]

The workplace can make a significant difference in this regard. A supportive work setting can help to reaffirm a sense of connectedness, whereas an unsupportive setting can reinforce feelings of isolation and estrangement.

What can also be important is managing the return to work for somebody who has been absent as a result of stress-related illness. (It has to be recognized that grief and trauma, while not necessarily producing an illness reaction, can very easily do so.) In an earlier work [38], I described an approach to preparation for an employee's return to work after a stress-related absence based on the following six questions:

- Which aspects of the situation are confidential and which can safely be shared with colleagues?
- Has the original problem gone away now or is it still there to be faced?
- Does the staff member have a balanced view of what led to the stress-related absence?
- What precise feelings is the member of staff experiencing?
- Will he or she require some degree of workload relief?
- What else needs to be done?

This framework can be a very useful one for helping somebody return to work and can therefore be very effective in providing an appropriate response.

Practice Focus 5.4

Len was attacked by a member of the public in the course of his duties. Although not seriously injured, he was absent from work for almost a month as a result of a mixture of shock and stress—a form of post-traumatic stress. Len was very anxious about returning to work and was quite fraught on the day he did return. This was not helped by two key factors:

i) he faced a huge backlog of work—no one had covered for him during his absence;

ii) while some colleagues were very supportive, others were quite insensitive and made jokes about the incident.

Len only lasted four days before going off sick again. Just over a week later he attempted to return again, but this time lasted only until lunch-time. He went home in tears and, six weeks later, he tendered his resignation. [38, p. 54]

Attig talks about how feelings of grief can lead to a person no longer feeling comfortable, no longer "at home":

> Our suffering includes "soul pain." I use *soul* to refer to that within us that sinks roots into the world, makes itself at home in our surroundings, finds nourishment and sustenance in the here and now of everyday life. When we suffer soul pain, we feel uprooted. We feel homesick. We feel estranged within and alienated from surroundings transformed by the death and our pain and anguish. We sense that we cannot find our way home to life as it was before the death. Fearing that we can never find our way to feeling at home again, we find it difficult to care about anything at all. [39, p. 37]

Again, the workplace can be crucial in this regard. By helping to establish a degree of normality and continuity, supportive colleagues and managers can be extremely helpful. However, if colleagues and managers "walk on eggshells" and fail to provide the degree of stability and security needed, they can make the situation worse rather than better.

One of the ways in which an organization can tackle these issues is through the sensitive and effective use of rituals, established patterns of social behavior that help people to "connect" with one another and reaffirm a sense of community and support. Gelfand et al. make apt comment when they argue that:

> Spirituality and religiosity, in whatever form observed, may hold particular importance at the end of life. Especially when the course of a terminal illness allows time for saying goodbye, mending relationships, and putting affairs in order, people often return to previous spiritual and religious roots or seek new connections. Families and communities faced with losses also often express the need to participate in spiritual or religious traditions as part of the communal grieving process. [24, p. 21]

Caring for the Caregivers

People who are regularly involved in supporting others who have experienced loss or trauma can be prone to what has come to be known as compassion fatigue. Warren [33] describes the following aspects or characteristics of compassion fatigue.

- Anxiety;
- Preoccupation with the trauma or the traumatized victim;
- Numbness or freezing response;
- Flashbacks (persistent arousal);
- Absorbs emotional suffering of others;
- Aches and pains (headaches, backaches, etc.);
- Changes in sleeping and eating patterns;
- Sweating or heart palpitations;
- Compromised immune system (increased susceptibility to illness);
- Sleep problems, nightmares, night terrors;
- Easily startled;
- Feelings of helplessness/hopelessness;
- Shock and/or denial;
- Hypervigilance;
- Poor concentration
- "Chicken Little syndrome" feeling of doom;
- Restrictive range of feelings.

This phenomenon presents a major challenge for organizations. This is because it is so easy for individuals to fall foul of compassion fatigue. It is as if the strain of supporting somebody who is grieving or traumatized produces a form of trauma in its own right. This can be linked with the discussion of vicarious traumatization discussed in Chapter 3.

Attig's work relating to caregivers is also important. This is because it has to be recognized that no-one can do another person's grieving for them:

> Caregivers should resist any temptation to attempt to do the difficult work of coping for us when we are bereaved. Our coping with loss is a personal experience, as is all coping. No other person can grieve for us. The challenges are ours to meet; the choices are ours to make. Yet, there is much that others can do for us as we relearn our worlds, find new places in our physical and social surroundings, learn how to continue to care about those who have died in their absence and struggle to find new, meaningful, and hopeful direction for our life stories. [15, p. 24]

It would be a serious mistake to fail to take seriously the concerns and need of the people who are providing care for others. There is a very real danger that, if such situations are not handled carefully, sensitively and appropriately, the result will be yet more pain, distress and suffering.

CONCLUSION

Of course, this chapter does not provide easy answers. In relation to such complex and demanding human problems as loss, grief and trauma, it would be a serious mistake indeed to oversimplify the situation to such an extent that we try to provide pat answers. The reality is that we need to wrestle with some very complex issues. To do this, we need to have a good understanding of what is possible and realistic. It is to be hoped that this chapter has given some guidance in that direction and provided a platform for further development of our understanding of these important matters.

One final point that is worth emphasizing is that, while providing care and support is clearly vitally important, we should, wherever possible, seek to go beyond this to make grief and trauma opportunities for growth and development [40]. This, of course, has to be done very carefully and sensitively if it is not to be a problem rather than a solution.

This chapter has outlined some important issues relating to how competent workplaces can make a positive contribution to staff well-being by offering care and support at times of loss and trauma. Chapter 6 builds on this by exploring what helps and what hinders when it comes to rising to the challenges presented by loss, grief and trauma in the workplace.

REFERENCES

1. B. Kahan, *Growing Up in Groups,* National Institute for Social Work/Her Majesty's Stationery Office, London, United Kingdom, 1994.
2. J. Bates and N. Thompson, Loss, Grief and Trauma in the Workplace, *Illness, Crisis & Loss, 15*(3), 2007.
3. N. Thompson, *Promoting Equality* (2nd Edition), Palgrave Macmillan, Basingstoke, United Kingdom and New York, 2003.
4. J. M. Schneider, *The Overdiagnosis of Depression: Recognizing Grief and Its Transformative Potential,* Seasons Press, Traverse City, Michigan, 2000.
5. H. Fitzgerald, *The Grieving Teen: A Guide for Teenagers and Their Friends,* Simon and Schuster, New York, 2000.
6. M. Stroebe and H. Schut, The Dual Process Model of Coping with Bereavement: Rationale and Description, *Death Studies, 23*(3), 1999.
7. L. A. DeSpelder and A. L. Strickland, Survivors' Guilt, in *Encyclopeadia of Death and Dying,* G. Howarth and O. Leaman (eds.), Routledge, London, United Kingdom, pp. 221-223, 2001.
8. P. C. Rosenblatt, Grief in Small-Scale Societies, in *Death and Bereavement Across Cultures,* C. M. Parkes P. Laungani, and B. Taylor (eds.), Routledge, London, United Kingdom, 1997.
9. U. Wikan, *Life among the Poor in Cairo,* Tavistock, London, United Kingdom, 1980.
10. U. Wikan, *Managing Turbulent Hearts: A Balinese Formula for Living,* University of Chicago Press, Chicago, Illinois, 1990.

11. T. L. Martin and K. J. Doka, *Men Don't Cry . . . Women Do: Transcending Gender Stereotypes of Grief,* Brunner/Mazel, Philadelphia, Pennsylvania, 2000.
12. J. Rick, S. O'Regan and A. Kinder, *Early Intervention Following Trauma: A Controlled Longitudinal Study at Royal Mail Group,* Institute for Employment Studies, Brighton, United Kingdom, 2006.
13. J. Rymaszewska and T. Philpot, *Reaching the Vulnerable Child: Therapy with Traumatized Children,* Jessica Kingsley Publishers, London, United Kingdom, 2006.
14. D. S. Everstine and L. Everstine, *Strategic Interventions for People in Crisis, Trauma, and Disaster* (Rev. Edition), Routledge, Abingdon, United Kingdom, 2006.
15. T. Attig, *How We Grieve: Relearning the World,* Oxford University Press, Oxford, United Kingdom and New York, 1996.
16. T. Attig, *The Heart of Grief: Death and the Search for Lasting Love,* Oxford University Press, Oxford, United Kingdom and New York, 2000.
17. A. Kellehear, *Compassionate Cities: Public Health and End-of-Life Care,* Routledge, London, United Kingdom and New York, 2005.
18. N. Thompson and D. Bevan, Death, Dying and Bereavement, in *The Blackwell Encyclopaedia of Social Work,* M. Davies (ed.), Blackwell, Oxford, United Kingdom, 2000.
19. N. Thompson, *People Problems,* Palgrave Macmillan, Basingstoke, United Kingdom and New York, 2006.
20. R. A. Neimeyer (ed.), *Meaning Reconstruction and the Experience of Loss,* American Psychological Association, Washington, DC, 2001.
21. R. A. Neimeyer and A. Anderson, Meaning Reconstruction Theory, in *Loss and Grief: A Guide for Human Services Practitioners,* N. Thompson (ed.), Palgrave Macmillan, Basingstoke, United Kingdom and New York, 2002.
22. J. Carol, *Journeys of Courage: Remarkable Stories of the Healing Power of Community,* Veritas, Dublin, Ireland, 2004.
23. F. Jameson, *Postmodernism, or, the Cultural Logic of Later Capitalism,* Duke University Press, Durham, North Carolina, 1991.
24. D. E. Gelfand, R. Raspa, S. H. Briller and S. M. Schim (eds.), *End-of-Life Stories: Crossing Disciplinary Boundaries,* Springer, New York, 2005.
25. B. D. Perry and M. Szalavitz, *The Boy Who Was Raised as a Dog and Other Stories from a Child Psychiatrist's Notebook,* Basic Books, New York, 2006.
26. M. F. Solomon and D. J. Siegal, *Healing Trauma: Attachment, Mind, Body and Brain,* W. W. Norton, New York, 2003.
27. N. Thompson, *Power and Empowerment,* Russell House Publishing, Lyme Regis, United Kingdom, 2007.
28. M. L. Crossley, *Introducing Narrative Psychology: Self, Trauma and the Construction of Meaning,* Open University Press, Maidenhead, United Kingdom, 2000.
29. M. Payne, *Narrative Therapy* (2nd Edition), Sage, London, United Kingdom and Thousand Oaks, California, 2006.
30. S. Myers, *Solution-Focused Approaches,* Russell House Publishing, Lyme Regis, United Kingdom, 2007.
31. N. Tehrani, *Workplace Trauma: Concepts, Assessments and Interventions,* Brunner-Routledge, Hove, United Kingdom, 2004.

32. G. S. Everly and J. T. Mitchell, *Critical Incident Stress Management (Cism): A New Era and Standard of Care in Crisis Intervention,* Chevron Publishing, Ellicott City, Maryland, 1999.
33. M. P. Warren, *From Trauma to Transformation,* Crown House, Carmarthen, United Kingdom, 2006.
34. M. Doel, *Using Groupwork,* Routledge, London, United Kingdom, 2005.
35. L. Hedtke and J. Winslade, *Re-membering Lives: Conversations with the Dying and the Bereaved,* Baywood, Amityville, New York, 2004.
36. S. McNamee and K. Gergen, *Relational Responsibility: Resources for Sustainable Dialogue,* Sage, Thousand Oaks, California, 1999.
37. R. A. Neimeyer, *Lessons of Loss: A Guide to Coping,* Center for the Study of Loss and Transition, Memphis, Tennessee, 2000.
38. N. Thompson, *Stress Matters,* Pepar Publications, Birmingham, United Kingdom, 1999.
39. T. Attig, Relearning the World: Making and Finding Meanings, in *Meaning Reconstruction and the Experience of Loss,* R. A. Neimeyer (ed.), American Psychological Association, Washington, DC, 2001.
40. J. M. Schneider with S. K. Zimmerman, *Transforming Loss: A Discovery Process,* Integra Press, East Lansing, Michigan, 2006.

CHAPTER 6

Helps and Hindrances

This chapter builds on discussions in the previous two chapters. Chapter 4 explored legal and policy issues that are important in establishing a community of caring in the workplace, while Chapter 5 built on those foundations to explore the broader issues of providing care and support. This chapter now takes the issues of support and care further by examining what helps and what hinders when it comes to dealing with loss, grief and trauma in the workplace. In doing so, it focuses on a range of practical steps that can help to promote good practice and gives guidance on how to take such matters forward. It also identifies potential pitfalls that can prevent progress or even, in some circumstances, make matters worse. The chapter is intended to be helpful and practical, based on sound theoretical understanding and experience, but not prescriptive in a simplistic way.

Before looking in any detail at the issues involved, it is important to be fully aware that, in addressing loss, grief and trauma in the workplace, we are dealing with some very fraught and difficult circumstances. While the pressures of such situations may push us in the direction of finding simple, straightforward remedies for the difficulties encountered, we have to be realistic enough to take on board the recognition that there will be no easy solutions. It is therefore understandable that we will make mistakes at times, that we will not always be able to achieve the outcomes we would like and that there may well be times when our efforts to help may accidentally make matters worse—at crisis points things can get significantly worse as well as significantly better, therefore the stakes can be very high. However, forewarned is forearmed. By developing a firm foundation of understanding, we can make an important contribution towards making sure that we are maximizing the chances of helping rather than hindering.

With this in mind, the chapter is divided into two main sections, one that examines what helps and one that explores what hinders. However, before we reach these two main sections, we shall be taking a slight detour. By this I mean that we shall first be considering a very helpful set of "Dos and Don'ts" drawn from the work of a highly respected writer and researcher in the loss and grief field, namely Robert Neimeyer. Neimeyer [1] helpfully identifies a range of possible responses to people who are grieving, some of which can be helpful (Dos) and some that can be significant hindrances (Don'ts). I shall list these, linking each one to the workplace and, where appropriate, adding additional comments about how these may relate to trauma situations (Neimeyer's focus is specifically on grief relating to bereavement).

DOS AND DON'TS WHEN REACHING OUT TO A MOURNER

Don't:
Force the mourner into a role, by saying "You're doing so well." Allow the mourner to have troubling feelings without the sense of letting you down.

It is understandable that colleagues and supervisors will want to be supportive and make positive comments. However, we also need to allow space for negative feelings to be aired. Where someone has been traumatized, this issue may arise a great deal as their memory may have been affected by the traumatic experience in such a way that they dwell on the negatives and may take time to establish a more balanced outlook on life.

Don't:
Tell the mourner what he or she "should" do. At best, this reinforces the mourner's sense of incompetence, and at worst, your advice can be "off target" completely.

When we see a colleague in distress or otherwise finding life difficult because of a loss, it is tempting to offer advice. However, as we saw in Chapter 5, this can be unhelpful. It is therefore a temptation to be resisted. This can be particularly difficult in the workplace where matters relating to quality of work may arise. When they do, they will need to be handled sensitively, as simply giving advice can be counterproductive (we shall return to this point below).

Don't:
Say, "Call me if you need anything." Vague offers are meant to be declined, and the mourner will pick up the cue that you implicitly hope he or she won't contact you.

It is important to make it clear that we are willing to support a grieving or traumatized colleague. Making the occasional vague comment is clearly not enough.

Don't:
Suggest that time heals all wounds. The wounds of loss never completely heal, and grief work is more active than this phrase suggests.

We can feel powerless to help someone who is immersed in grief or trauma and this, if we are not careful, can lead to making comments that are more about reassuring ourselves than the person we are trying to help. We cannot take a person's pain away and it is pointless to try to do so. Our efforts are best directed elsewhere (see Chapter 5 plus the "What helps?" section below).

> Don't:
> Delegate helping to others. Your personal presence and concern will make a difference.

An important part of creating a supportive work environment is for everyone to show genuine concern. Anyone who opts out of this is likely to give the (perhaps unintentional) message that they do not care. As we shall see below, a supportive *community* (including the workplace community) is an important part of helping.

> Don't:
> Say "I know how you feel." Each griever's experience of grief is unique, so invite the mourner to share his or her feelings, rather than presuming that you know what the issues are for that person.

Expressing empathy is important, but this needs to be done in a way that respects the individual circumstances of the person concerned and not in a blanket fashion. We do not know how someone else feels. Even if you have had a very similar experience yourself, that person's feelings may not coincide with yours. Implying that your feelings are indeed the same as his or hers can be seen to devalue the unique experiences of your grieving or traumatized colleague.

> Don't:
> Use hackneyed consolation, by saying, "There are other fish in the sea" or "God works in mysterious ways." This only convinces the mourner that you do not care enough to understand.

This again can give a colleague a misleading message that you do not care and that you are more concerned with playing down the significance of the situation than with being genuinely supportive. Helping involves being understanding and sweeping comments imply that we do not know enough about the specifics of this individual's circumstances to be able to understand and be supportive.

> Don't:
> Try to hurry the person through grief by urging that he or she get busy, give away the deceased's possessions, etc. Grief work takes time and patience and cannot be done on a fixed schedule.

A grieving or traumatized individual will need to work at their own pace, and so allowances may need to be made in terms of expected quality or quantity of work. Expecting too much too soon can be counterproductive and may even be quite harmful. If grief or trauma issues are causing concern about quality or quantity of work, then this situation will need to be handled carefully and sensitively. Hurrying someone along will not help.

Do:

Open the door to communication. If you aren't sure what to say, ask, "How are you feeling today?" or "I've been thinking about you. How is it going today?"

Communication and information provision are important foundations of a caring workplace community. Communication helps people to connect with one another, both practically and spiritually, and this can be of immense value at a time of loss or trauma. Poor or non-existent communication, by contrast, can reinforce a sense of isolation and alienation.

Do:

Listen 80% of the time, and talk 20% of the time. Very few people take the time to listen to someone's deepest concerns. Be one of the few. Both you and the mourner are likely to learn as a result.

The theme of leadership has arisen at various points in this book. Effective listening is a key part of leadership, and this applies especially to people who are grieving or traumatized and have thus been destabilized in some way. The importance of listening is emphasized below.

Do:

Offer specific help and take the initiative to call the mourner. If you also respect the survivor's privacy, your concrete assistance with the demands of daily living will be appreciated.

In Chapter 4 we noted the importance of making information available and offering help, as it is recognized that people who are grieving may be reluctant to ask for help. As Doka comments:

> It is more helpful to be specific in your help—offering, for example, to assist them with work, or helping with child care or a meal—rather than simply saying, "Call me," or, "Can I help?" Bereaved persons may be reluctant to seek help or even be too confused and disorientated to assess what they need. [2, p. 12]

This will also apply to traumatized individuals.

Do:

Expect future "rough spots" with active attempts at coping with difficult feelings and decisions for months following the loss.

Workplaces commonly underestimate how long grieving is likely to last and how intense it is likely to be [2]. We therefore have to be careful not to make this mistake. Having unrealistic expectations will serve only to make the situation worse.

Do:

"Be there" for the mourner. There are few rules for helping aside from openness and caring.

"Being there" may sound like a cliché, but it is nonetheless important to give a clear message that, while a colleague is going through stormy seas, we can do our best to provide an anchoring point—something that may be greatly appreciated later when the situation has settled.

> *Do:*
> *Talk about your own losses and how you adapted to them. Although the mourner's coping style may be different from your own, your self-disclosure will help.*

Talking about our own losses (or indeed experiences of trauma) can help to make it clear that loss is an inevitable part of life and a challenge that we all face and that trauma is also a common human experience. "Connecting" with one another in this way by talking about our own losses, if handled sensitively, can be very helpful.

> *Do:*
> *Use appropriate physical contact—like an arm around the shoulder or a hug—when words fail. Learn to be comfortable with shared silence, rather than chattering away in an attempt to cheer the person up.*

Touch is, of course, an important element of non-verbal communication. It can play a key role in establishing an ethos of support if used appropriately.

> *Do:*
> *Be patient with the griever's story, and allow him or her to share memories of the lost loved one. This fosters a healthy continuity as the person orients to a changed future.*

In Chapter 2 we noted the significance of "narrative," of maintaining a thread of meaning and developing new stories that are consistent with our new circumstances. The workplace is an important part of the context for such a narrative. (The italicized comments are taken from Neimeyer [1, p. 63].)

HELPING

In Chapter 4, the point was emphasized that we should not underestimate the important role of having policies in place and an organizational culture that supports them. The leadership challenge of having a culture that makes such policies a reality, rather than simply papers on a shelf gathering dust, is a key to making sure that helping is a primary focus of what we do. We also noted in Chapter 5 that there are various ways in which help can be offered. What is presented here under the heading of "Helping" can therefore be seen as an extension and, to a certain extent, a consolidation of how organizations and the individuals within them can play a positive role in responding to the demands that loss, grief and trauma make of us.

Understanding

When it comes to helping, what is very important is making sure that people are *understanding*—in both senses of the word. That is, people involved need to have a degree of knowledge and understanding and it is, of course, a primary role of this book to go some way towards providing the understanding necessary. In addition to this, people need to be understanding, in the sense of being appreciative of the difficulties involved; they need to be able to show appropriate empathy in dealing with the challenges of supporting people.

An example of the first form of understanding is discussed by Schiraldi in relation to trauma:

> We can temporarily escape a traumatic memory by separating and walling off the memory. Instead of being smoothly connected to all other memories, the highly charged traumatic memories become dissociated or isolated. While the memory may be walled off for awhile, it is not filed in long-term memory. Instead of taking its place alongside other memories on file, the traumatic memory remains "on the desktop" where it repeatedly intrudes upon awareness and cannot, it seems, be put away for long. Dissociated traumatic memory material is said to be walled off, split off, fragmented, separated off, or compartmentalized such that the information does not become integrated with the rest of one's memory material, nor is it fully connected to present awareness. [3, p. 14]

This means that someone who has been traumatized may continue to have vivid memories of the traumatic event, a process that can lead to considerable distress. If key people in an employing organization are not aware of this, they may misread the situation and thereby mishandle it. This does not mean that there is an expectation that managers and colleagues will become experts in trauma or related matters, but it is important to recognize that an understanding of at least the basics is required, along with a willingness to find out more when the relevant circumstances arise.

Practice Focus 6.1

Li was very concerned to learn that his colleague, Sandro, had been assaulted and robbed on his way home from a concert he attended. He wanted to be as supportive of Sandro as he could. However, he had not bargained for how much Sandro would be affected by the incident. He lost his confidence, became quite withdrawn and seemed to be frightened of his own shadow. He managed to get through his work, although both quantity and quality suffered in the aftermath of the incident. Li thought that the situation would rectify itself after a few days, that Sandro would return to his old self once he had had chance to "work things through his system." But, as those few days turned into a few weeks, Li became increasingly concerned. He began to wonder whether Sandro had been traumatized by the attack and, if so, what this would mean for the help he might need. Consequently, Li took it upon himself to find out more about trauma and its effects. He began with some information downloaded from the Internet and this led him into reading a number of books on the subject. The more he read, the more he realized how ill-equipped he has been in trying to help Sandro without having a proper understanding of the complex issues involved.

Part of the second form of understanding is active listening, being able to show that we are concerned enough to want to help people deal with their plight. Listening is something that we have to keep doing. It is not something that we can simply do once and then switch off from, particularly in dealing with people who have been traumatized. They may need to go over more than once what has happened to them. In fact, this type of repetition can be helpful provided that it does not become what is referred to as "rumination"—that is, the tendency to get stuck in negative thoughts about the situation.

It is also possible to combine the two types of understanding—for example, by being aware of the signs that a person is grieving. This shows both an understanding of the knowledge base relating to loss and grief and a sensitivity to what people may be going through. This is important because, as we noted in Chapter 1, grief arises from a wide variety of loss situations and not just from bereavement. We therefore need to be "tuned in" to how grief can manifest itself even when no death has occurred. In this regard, the list of effects of grief provided by Rawson is instructive:

- Shock
- Numbness
- Severe cold
- Unreality
- Euphoria
- Exhaustion
- Depression
- Sadness
- Sorrow
- Aches and pains
- Seeing/feeling/hearing/smelling the person who has died
- Not feeling anything at all, even pain
- Sleeplessness
- Not wanting "to go on"
- Despair
- Loss of appetite
- Anxiety
- Restlessness
- Inability to concentrate
- Inability to make decisions

- Inability to express yourself
- Inability to be creative
- Churning stomach
- Tearfulness
- Tearlessness
- Guilt
- Relief
- Illness
- Small tasks seeming like mountains
- Time dragging
- Proneness to accidents and dropping things
- Muscle weakness
- Blurred vision
- Nightmares
- Suicidal feelings
- Nothing matters
- A heavy feeling
- Light-headedness
- Freedom
- Needing to go over and over the last days/weeks/hours/minutes
- Needing to talk with others, especially those who know what the deceased means to you. [4, pp. 24-26]

Individual items from this list will not necessarily be a cause for concern in their own right, but where a pattern begins to develop, it may be giving a clear message that the person concerned is grieving. This does not mean that they will need help, for, as we have noted earlier, grieving is not in itself an indication that help is needed, but in the workplace, it can be helpful to know when someone is grieving, as it may be necessary to make allowances or, at the very least, to give a clear message of support so that silence on the subject on the part of employers is not interpreted as an uncaring attitude.

Practice Focus 6.2

Katherine was a highly valued worker whose talents and commitment could not be questioned. However, at one point, the standards of her work dropped significantly. She seemed preoccupied, lost her appetite, seemed constantly close to tears and was very unlike her usual self in a number of other ways. Sinead, her line manager, was convinced that she was grieving and was so concerned that she took it upon herself to raise the subject with Katherine and ask her outright whether someone close to her had died. Her response to the question was short and to the point: "No." She clearly didn't want to talk about her personal circumstances. However, a few days later, Katherine made a significant mistake that could have cost her company a lot of money (and embarrassment) if a colleague had not spotted the error and rectified it. As a result of this, Sinead felt the need to press the issue with her. She therefore said to Katherine "I don't know what is troubling you and I respect your right to confidentiality, but we need to do something to make sure that whatever is bothering you does not lead to problems." At this point Katherine realized she couldn't keep things to herself any longer. She therefore explained that her parents had split up after over 40 years together and that this had hit her quite hard as she had had no inkling of any relationship problems. Sinead then realized that Katherine was indeed grieving—grieving for the idealized perfect relationship she thought her parents had—even though no one had died. She recognized that she had made a mistake in assuming that grief arises only in response to a death.

Not Disenfranchising Grief

Reference was made earlier in the book to the notion of disenfranchised grief, where grieving is not socially recognized or supported in certain circumstances. It can be very helpful if we can do whatever we reasonably can to challenge such disenfranchisement. There are various ways in which this can happen. In relation to each of the three kinds of disenfranchisement identified by Doka [5], we can try to avoid the negative effects of disenfranchisement, as the following examples illustrate:

- *The relationship is disenfranchised.* It is important that grief arising from unconventional relationships is not disregarded. In particular, from the point of view of valuing diversity and promoting equality, it is important to ensure that prejudice against same-sex relationships is not allowed to stand in the way of an individual's grieving.
- *The loss is disenfranchised.* Similarly, it is important to make sure that grief arising from losses that may be stigmatized (by some people at least) in some way— for example, AIDS-related deaths or deaths by suicide—is treated any less supportively.
- *The griever is disenfranchised.* Older workers and/or staff who have a developmental disability should, or course, be given as much right to grieve as any other worker.

A further aspect of disenfranchised grief is, as Corr [6] points out, the fact that the workplace itself can be a source of disenfranchisement—that is, the workplace can be seen as a "taboo" place when it comes to grief.

Avoiding Triggers

There will be certain "triggers" that can set off a traumatic or distressing reaction for example. Examples of this would be painful reminders of a loss that may occur at a particular time; alternately, particular dates, such as anniversaries of a key person's death, may be significant for the individual who has experienced the loss, and allowances may need to be made for that. What can be very helpful, therefore, is doing everything we reasonably can to reduce or remove such triggers. What counts as a "trigger" will, of course, vary from person to person, situation to situation, so it is not possible to generalize. However, a useful question that we can ask ourselves is: In these particular circumstances, what may prove distressing for this particular individual and what can we reasonably do to avoid problems arising? It may be that there is nothing we can do at times, that there is no reasonable way of avoiding the trigger arising. However, it is nonetheless worthwhile exploring the possibility of doing so where feasible.

Promoting Growth

The point has already been made that grief and trauma can, despite being very painful experiences, produce situations where there can be significant personal growth and development. Schneider offers helpful comments in this regard:

> There are several key elements which, if fulfilled, help people find a transformative path through their grief:
>
> • The need to feel cared for, secure, protected and loved;
> • The need for validation at times of transition and loss;
> • The need for a challenge when a loss becomes our only important identity;
> • The need for facilitative environments—places of sanctuary and therapeutic communities;
> • The need for play and humor to have a role in the healing process;
> • The need to ultimately find a source of nurturance, validation, forgiveness and adventure from within. [7, p. 28]

We should not assume that all loss and trauma experiences will produce such growth, but the potential is clearly there. If colleagues are aware of this potential, they may be in a position to help provide an environment in which such growth can take place. However, it is important that such steps, if taken, are handled sensitively and carefully.

Personalizing the Loss

We have already noted the significant role of meaning making in relation to grief and trauma. It is this central role of meaning that makes each experience of grief unique to the individual concerned. For example, while two people who work together may both lose their father in the same week, how each of them experiences that loss may be entirely different. For one person, there may be a sense of devastating loss, as the death was entirely unexpected (as the result of an accident perhaps). For the other, however, the death may come as a relief following the slow, painful and heartbreaking decline of a proud man who has been battling against a very debilitating cancer.

Such individual reactions are to be expected; the idea that people's grieving follows a standard pattern is a dangerous myth (see the discussion of stages of grief below), as it fails to account for the huge differences in people's experiences in the aftermath of a loss (or indeed a trauma). What is needed, then, is an approach to each individual that takes account of the specific circumstances of the situation and not one that overgeneralizes or fails to respect the uniqueness of the person concerned. An important part of this, as was acknowledged earlier, will be a willingness to *listen*. This will help us to understand the situation from the point of view of the person we are seeking to help and not try to impose our own definition of the situation and need to be done.

Seeing the Loss in Context

Kellehear emphasizes the role of community in relation to loss and grief. He offers a significant insight in commenting that:

> Frequently we leave death and loss to the psychological professions and in this way support the falsity that death is an individual and private matter. Or we hand the problem of mortality to hospice and palliative care, giving them, and anyone else who looks on, the equally false impression that end-of-life care is merely terminal care, care in the final weeks and days of life. In these two professional storylines we no longer speak about the universality of loss or the commonplace ordinariness of death, dying and loss. And except for significant disasters, we seldom recognize every individual's death and loss as a community experience. [8, pp. viii–ix]

While there are clearly personal, intimate aspects to any significant loss, this does not alter the fact that death is as much a sociological phenomenon as it is psychological—that is, we need to consider the social aspects as well as the personal or psychological ones. The community dimension is a crucial part of that.

Part of the notion of community is a shared symbolism that gives a sense of connectedness. Rituals can be seen as an important part of that symbolism. Doka's comments are helpful in this regard:

> ritual reaffirms community. It offers an opportunity for the different strands of a community, potentially fragmented by a crisis, to stand together and publicly demonstrate their fundamental unity. [9, p. 180]

Rituals can be understood as a form of symbolic holding hands or linking arms, standing firm and united against the challenges of adversity. As such, they are an important underpinning of resilience. Their role and significance should not be underestimated.

HINDERING

Reference was made earlier to the way in which the tensions involved in grief and trauma situations can lead some people into avoidance behaviors where they try to sweep the problem under the carpet in order to be able to pretend it is not there. This sort of approach is very unproductive and can also be quite harmful insofar as it can give a clear message (albeit an unintended one) that we do not care, that we are not being supportive. This can seriously add to the difficulties an individual or a group of peoople may be facing. It is therefore important to be aware of the various ways in which our actions (or inactions) can be counterproductive. My comments here should help to lay a foundation for developing such understanding.

A "One Size Fits All" Approach

We should be very wary of falling into the trap of adopting too inflexible an approach. We have to recognize that there will be significant differences in terms of how people respond to loss or trauma. While there are common patterns, as discussed in Chapter 5 under the heading of "Typical Patterns of Grieving," we also have to be aware that such broad patterns are subject to considerable variation in terms of such factors as culture and gender. It is also important to consider how generational factors are very relevant, too. For example, Riches and Dawson [10, p. 85] give significant food for thought when they comment that:

> Kandt [11] argues that adolescents generally lack the life experience that teaches them that they can survive trauma. As yet they have not experienced the insight that no matter how bad events seem, eventually they move on and can in time, seem more manageable.

What we have, then, is a complex picture that incorporates both psychological and sociological factors. Rejecting a "one size fits all" approach is in some ways the other side of the coin to personalizing the loss, as discussed earlier. However, it goes beyond this to recognize that there will be not only individual differences in grief reactions, but also group or cohort differences in terms of such social factors as gender, ethnicity and age expectations.

Medicalization

Another significant hindrance worthy of consideration can be a tendency to "medicalize" the situation. That is, we can have significant problems where people regard the effects of grief and trauma as symptoms of an illness. We have to remember that, when peoople use terms such as symptoms and treatment, these should, at best, be used in a metaphorical sense only. In fact, there is a strong argument that they should not be used at all, because they can have the effect of being quite disempowering. It is therefore important that we should not adopt an uncritical medical perspective on what are in reality very complex, multi-level, psychological, social and organizational issues.

Writing on the topic of trauma arising from abuse, Briere [12, p. 126] makes an important point in arguing that:

> The notion that abuse-related behavior is not reflective of illness potentially increases the survivor's sense of self-control (as opposed to control by a disease process), and removes the stigma inherent in being defined in terms of pathology. Sadly, clinicians who adhere to a medical model when working with abuse survivors can do the reverse: by referring to "symptoms" and "disorders" when describing abuse sequelae, they can further complicate or intensify client stigmatization.

To reject medicalization is not by any means to play down the significance of grief and trauma and the devastating harm they can do to a person's well-being. Nor is it to deny that a medical perspective has no place in our overall understanding of the subject. What is being rejected is the uncritical acceptance of very complex, multi-level problems as simply signs of an illness or underlying pathology.

Practice Focus 6.3

Paul was a confident and experienced firefighter who enjoyed his work and felt proud of how important it was. However, after being involved in an incident in which he witnessed two children die as a result of being trapped inside a burning building, he experienced a severe traumatic reaction. The incident really knocked him out of his stride and he found it extremely difficult to get back to normal and feel comfortable at work again. His employers were very supportive and offered him individual counseling. He was also fortunate enough to be able to attend a local support group. However, one aspect of the help that he received that made him quite dissatisfied was the constant use of medical terminology. He did not see himself as ill, as there was nothing physically wrong with him and he certainly wasn't happy about having the label "mental illness" applied to him. He had enough insight to realize that he was going through a perfectly understandable (albeit difficult, painful and highly distressing) reaction to a horrific experience. He resented professionals trying to package what he was going through into neat "symptoms" of some sort of "disorder": "You try going through what I did and see how you feel when people try to make out you are ill or 'disordered'" was what he was very tempted to say on a number of occasions.

Frueh, Elhai and Kaloupeck, in discussing research relating to trauma, also raise concerns about the dangers of conceiving of human distress as symptoms of an illness:

> Such findings raise the concern that we should not rush to apply psychiatric labels to what may be relatively brief and normal human reactions in the face of tragic events. Put another way: most humans appear to be far less fragile than many mental health professionals anticipate. [13, p. 68]

This is particularly important in the workplace where the actions and attitudes of colleagues and indeed of the organization as a whole can be vitally important in shaping how well a person copes, the extent and intensity of distress experienced, the development of resilience and opportunities for growth and development. Oversimplifying the situation in this way (that is, by conceptualizing what is happening to a grieving or traumatized individual as symptoms of a putative illness) bypasses these highly important issues and fails to appreciate the central role of the social context of grief and trauma—specifically the workplace dimensions of this context.

Offering Simple Advice

We should also remember Attig's concern, noted earlier, that we should not be offering simple responses to people's problems, as this can be quite counter-productive. Such advice can be unwelcome and give a message that implies that our role is to govern and direct rather than support and facilitate. It can also give the (perhaps misleading) message that we are trying to take control—see the discussion below of "Taking Control."

Putting People under Pressure to "Let Go"

Attig [14] is also helpful in reminding us that we would be very unwise to put people under pressure to "let go." In Chapter 1, reference was made to the importance of understanding that it can be a significant mistake to think in terms of healthy grieving involving "letting go" of the person or thing that is lost. A much more helpful approach is to think about making a transition, so that the relationship with the person or thing no longer takes its previous form, but still exists in a very meaningful way. Attig explains this clearly in the following terms:

> We need not break our bonds with the deceased but instead redefine the nature of those bonds and their places in our lives. Rather than challenging us to separate from the dead, their deaths challenge us to maintain meaningful connection and to integrate redefined relationships in our necessarily new life patterns. [14, p. 174]

Maintaining our "bonds" with the person or thing we have lost means that who or what we have lost can continue to play a meaningful role in our lives. This is an important process that should not be discouraged as a result of a lack of understanding of the nature of grief.

Silverman gives a telling example of how pervasive (and how damaging) the idea of "letting go" has become:

One of my students provided another example of how pervasive the concept of "letting go" is. He told me about an assignment he was given as a psychology student at another school the year before. When asked to write a paper on an experience that most influenced his life, he wrote about his mother's death five years earlier. His professor did not mark the paper. Instead, he told the student that his description of the death was too vivid, given the time that had passed, and that he should have let it go a long time ago. He suggested that the student see a therapist as soon as possible. My student was stunned and dropped the course. [15, p 208]

This type of prescriptive approach based on a superficial and misleading understanding of this aspect of grief can do a lot of harm by putting people under pressure to "let go" rather than supporting them (or at least just giving them space) to integrate their loss into their lives and their understanding of their lives.

Expecting People to Grieve in Stages

On a similar theme, the points made earlier in Chapter 2 about the rejection of models of grieving that are based on stages should provide ample warning that it is dangerous to put people under pressure to grieve according to such stages. However well meaning it may be to try and indicate to somebody that they should be moving to a new stage, it is unsound both theoretically and ethically to do so. It is therefore not a helpful thing to do. The following passage from Hooyman and Kramer casts further light on this:

> What is important is the meaning to us of that loss. It is not necessary for the loss to be recognized or validated by others for us to experience grief. Accordingly, no two people grieve in the same way. Each person's grief process differs in intensity, duration and time to resolution (Kagawa-Singer [16]). Although stage theories of grief are now generally rejected (Klass [17, 18]; Walter [19]), a constellation of feelings typically accompanies a significant loss. These are fear, including the fear of expressing one's feelings, numbness and shock, dread, anxiety, guilt, anger, rage, and intense sadness [20, pp. 16-17].

So, while there may be elements in common across people's experiences of grief, it is a mistake to oversimplify the variability of grief responses by assuming that they follow (or should follow) set stages or patterns.

Taking this point a step further, Riches and Dawson [10] refer to the work of Wortman and Silver who have identified a number of bereavement myths. It is important in trying to deal with grief issues, therefore, that we should be aware of these myths and make sure that we do not succumb to any of them:

> A major contribution to this debate [about the myths of bereavement therapy] was made by Wortman and Silver [21] whose summary of empirical evidence challenged what they called the dominant "myths" of bereavement

therapy. In reviewing what they claimed was the best research (methodologically speaking), they presented the following observations:

- intense distress and/or depression is far from inevitable following bereavement;
- no link has been demonstrated between intensity of grieving and subsequent resolution;
- on the contrary, those who seemed most distressed during early stages of loss were more likely to be distressed, one to two years later and, apart from one study, there is little evidence that "suppressed" grief causes problems later in life;
- there is no obvious relationship between the intensity of parental attachment and levels of distress following Sudden Infant Death Syndrome;
- preoccupation with the reality of the loss, as demonstrated by high levels of rumination, appears to place bereaved people at greater risk of poor mental and physical outcomes later in life;
- "resolution" of grief, as measured either by return to normal functioning or in being able to "come to terms" with the death is *never* achieved for significant numbers of bereaved people. Indeed where death is sudden, unexpected or in tragic circumstances, most people appear incapable of finding any satisfying explanation. [21, p. 33]

The existence of such misleading myths, plus the common misunderstanding that people should grieve in stages adds up to a situation which should make us wary of relying on "folk wisdom" about loss and grief. This reinforces the point made above about the importance of *understanding*, in the sense of having a good, well-informed appreciation of the issues involved when someone experiences a significant loss.

Trying to Cheer People Up

It is understandable that, when encountering people who have experienced, or are still experiencing considerable pain and distress, we will wish to try and cheer them up, to try and introduce a lighter and more positive note into their day. However, this can be potentially disastrous. This is because it may communicate the message that we are not recognizing their pain; we are not prepared to engage with the difficulties they face in their world at this moment, and that we want them to cheer up so that *we* can feel better. This amounts to saying that our own feelings are more important than theirs, and that is clearly not a helpful thing to say. This is not to say that we have to be negative and morbid about such situations, but simplistically trying to cheer somebody up is clearly doomed to failure. If we are going to try and balance out positives and negatives, this has to be done in a very skillful and sensitive way.

Taking Control

People who are grieving or traumatized will often experience a strong sense of powerlessness. If we are not careful, our good intentions can unwittingly make this situation worse if we try and take control.

Transactional analysis helps us to realize that there is a powerful dynamic that can develop that can prove quite destructive [22]. It involves a grieving or traumatized person feeling distressed and powerless and therefore presenting as, in some ways, a child-like figure (in the sense of appearing vulnerable and in need of support or protection). This can evoke a parental-type response from colleagues or other concerned parties. While this is an understandable response, it runs the risk of reinforcing the sense of powerlessness. That is, the more parental we are, the more child-like and vulnerable the person we are trying to support is likely to feel. It can also very easily be perceived by the person on the receiving end of it as paternalistic and thus unhelpful.

From this we can see that it is important to resist the temptation to take control, as this is likely to be more of a hindrance than a help.

As a footnote to this, we need to bear in mind, that, in exceptional circumstances we may have to take control. For example, if someone's behavior presents health and safety risks (as a result of being in a confused state of mind, for example), then it may be necessary to take control to ensure their, or other people's, safety. However, such steps should be seen as a last resort and not as a usual option.

Workplace Cultures

Finally, in terms of hindrance, we should take account of the fact that some workplace cultures can be very unhelpful if they are of the wrong sort. For example, Schneider talks about the ways in which post-traumatic growth and transformational grief can be held back by a number of factors, not least the culture in which people are operating:

> grieving is universally accepted as a necessary human response when something important is lost. The potential to grow from it, however, is often limited by the degree of oppression, poverty, and cultural sanctions experienced. [23, p. xvii]

Workplace cultures, including the range of sanctions they incorporate, are very powerful influences on behavior and interactions. They are also a strong shaper of the emotional climate within a particular workplace, and this can be a significant factor in terms of how emotional issues are dealt with. For example, in some cultures, emotional expression can be strongly discouraged—it becomes taboo to voice any emotional concerns that may be experienced by others as unsettling. In such an environment, a grieving or traumatized person is likely to feel isolated, unsupported and even alienated—pretty much the exact opposite of what they are likely to need to be feeling at that time. This type of culture can therefore be not only unhelpful but actually harmful.

Shaping workplace cultures is an important feature of leadership, and so this question of culture is one to which we shall return in Chapter 7 where we explore the vital role of leadership.

Practice Focus 6.4

Jack was a police officer and his wife, Anita, was a social worker. They were both involved in responding to a disaster in which over 100 people were killed. It was difficult, demanding and distressing work for both of them. The great irony, though, was that Jack received far more support in dealing with the situation than Anita did. Anita was quite disappointed that, despite being employed in the caring professions, there was relatively little caring going on when it came to her own support needs. Her employers seemed to take the attitude that she was paid to do her job and she should get on with it. Even though there was a very strong emphasis on being supportive towards clients, there was no culture of staff care, no real commitment to promoting well-being among employees. Jack's experiences were quite different. While the police force had a reputation for being tough and robust when it came to law enforcement, the culture within the organization featured a very strong commitment to staff care. The key word they used was loyalty: "We expect loyalty from our officers and we show loyalty in return when it is needed" was how one senior officer put it. These differences in workplace culture made a huge difference to how Jack and Anita felt about their respective experiences in responding to the same crisis.

CONCLUSION

This chapter has provided a broad overview of some of the main helps and hindrances that we need to be aware of if we are to tackle loss, grief and trauma in the workplace in a meaningful way that stands a reasonable chance of being effective. When it comes to "helps," we have been able to see that there are various ways in which colleagues and managers in particular and organizations in general can be of assistance to people who are gong through a very difficult period in their lives (as indeed we all will sooner or later). When it comes to hindrances, we have also seen how many different ways we can do more harm than good if we are not "tuned in" to the dangers involved. While the list of potential hindrances may appear a little daunting at first, the positive message is that "forewarned is forearmed"—that is, by becoming more aware of these pitfalls, we are far less likely to fall into to them.

The chapter has provided a blend of theory and practice, insofar as it has distilled a number of practice guidelines from the extensive theory base relating to loss, grief and trauma in general, but specifically tailored to the issues that arise in the workplace.

In some ways, this chapter has brought together and consolidated issues discussed in other chapters, while also adding new ideas and insights. In doing this, it has helped to pull together important themes and prepare the way for the concluding chapter. Chapter 7 will therefore build on this by identifying the key lessons to be learned and the recurring themes that we will need to bear in mind as we take our understanding forward.

REFERENCES

1. R. A. Neimeyer, *Lessons of Loss: A Guide to Coping*, Center for the Study of Loss and Transition, Memphis, Tennessee, 2000.
2. K. Doka, A Primer on Loss and Grief, in *Living with Grief: At Work, at School, at Worship*, in J. D. Davidson and K. J. Doka (eds.), Hospice Foundation of America, Brunner/Mazel, Washington, DC, 1999.
3. G. R. Schiraldi, *The Post-Traumatic Stress Disorder Sourcebook: A Guide to Healing, Recovery and Growth*, McGraw-Hill, New York, 1999.
4. P. Rawson, *Grappling with Grief: A Guide for the Bereaved*, Karnac, London, United Kingdom, 2005.
5. K. J. Doka, *Disenfranchised Grief: Recognizing Hidden Sorrow*, Lexington, Lexington, Massachusetts, 1989.
6. C. Corr, Enhancing the Concept of Disenfranchised Grief (presentation to the annual meeting of the Association for Death Education and Counseling, Chicago, Illinois, 1998), cited in *Living with Grief at Work, at School, at Worship*, J. D. Davidson and K. J. Doka (eds.), Hospice Foundation of America, Brunner/Mazel, Washington, DC, 1999.
7. J. Schneider with S. K. Zimmerman, *Transforming Loss: A Discovery Process*, Integra, East Lansing, Michigan, 2006.
8. A. Kellehear, *Compassionate Cities: Public Health and End-of-Life Care*, Routledge, London, United Kingdom and New York, 2005.
9. K. J. Doka, Memorialization, Ritual, and Public Tragedy, in *Living with Grief: Coping with Public Tragedy*, M. Lattanzi-Licht and K. J. Doka (eds.), Hospice Foundation of America/Brunner-Routledge, Washington, DC, 2003.
10. G. Riches and P. Dawson, *An Intimate Loneliness: Supporting Bereaved Parents and Siblings*, Open University Press, Buckingham, United Kingdom, 2000.
11. V. Kandt, Adolescent Bereavement: Turning a Fragile Time into Acceptance and Peace, *The School Counselor, 41*(3), pp. 203-211, 1999.
12. J. N. Briere, *Child Abuse Trauma: Theory and Treatment of the Lasting Effects*, Sage, New York, 1992.
13. B. C. Frueh, J. D. Elhai and D. G. Kaloupeck, Unresolved Issues in the Assessment of Trauma Exposure and Posttraumatic Reactions, in *Posttraumatic Stress Disorder: Issues and Controversies*, G. M. Rosen (ed.), John Wiley and Sons, Chichester, United Kingdom, 2004
14. T. Attig, *How We Grieve: Relearning the World*, Oxford University Press, Oxford, United Kingdom and New York, 1996.

15, P. R. Silverman, *Never Too Young to Know: Death in Children's Lives,* Oxford University Press, Oxford, United Kingdom, 2000.
16. M. Kagawa-Singer and L. J. Blackhall, The Cultural Context of Death Rituals and Mourning Practices, *Oncology Nursing Forum, 29*(5), pp. 1752-1756, 2001.
17. D. Klass, The Deceased Child in the Psychic and Social Worlds of Bereaved Parents During the Resolution of Grief, in *Continuing Bonds: New Understandings of Grief,* D. Klass, P. R. Silverman and S. L. Nickman (eds.), Taylor & Francis, Washington, DC, 1996.
18. D. Klass, Developing a Cross-Cultural Model of Grief: The State of the Field, *Omega, 39*(3), pp. 153-178, 1999.
19. C. A. Walter, *The Loss of a Life Partner,* Columbia University Press, New York, 2003.
20. N. R. Hooyman and B. J. Kramer, *Living Through Loss: Interventions Across the Life Span,* Columbia University Press, New York, 2006.
21. C. B. Wortman and R. C. Silver, The Myths of Coping with Loss, *Journal of Consulting and Clinical Psychology, 57,* pp. 349-357, 1989.
22. E. Berne, *Games People Play: The Psychology of Human Relationships,* Penguin, Harmondsworth, United Kingdom, 1970.
23. J. Schneider, *The Overdiagnosis of Depression: Recognizing Grief and its Transformative Potential,* Seasons Press, Traverse City, Michigan, 2000.

CHAPTER 7
Conclusion

This book has presented a wide-ranging discussion of some very complex issues. The first three chapters focused primarily, but not exclusively, on the theoretical underpinnings of our subject area, while Chapters 4 to 6 focused mainly on the practical implications, both the broader policy issues and the more specific actions that we can take (and those that we need to avoid taking) in order to respond to the challenges of loss, grief and trauma in the workplace. This final chapter now summarizes, consolidates and, to some degree, extends some of the key arguments and points presented in the book and aims to provide food for thought in relation to taking the issues forward positively and constructively.

The key elements can be identified in the following statements:

- The workplace is a *human* environment. A *people* focus must therefore be at the heart of our endeavors.
- Meaning is a key factor. We must therefore give careful consideration to the question of *spirituality*.
- *Leadership* is a crucial requirement. We are unlikely to succeed without the development of high-quality leadership as a focus for our efforts.
- Providing "care" is not enough—*empowerment* and *growth* are also important aims to pursue.
- Loss, grief and trauma are profoundly personal, but they are also *community* issues. The workplace is a key part of that community context.

We shall now explore each of these five key areas in more detail.

THE HUMAN DIMENSION
OF ORGANIZATIONAL LIFE

Successful organizations need to address a number of important concerns if they are to remain successful. These will include financial and technical matters; operational and strategic concerns; and various related matters. However, even more important than all of these will be issues relating to the *people* dimension of the organization—what tends to be referred to these days as "human resources." Unless organizations handle the people dimension effectively, they will experience many problems. There is no doubt that people are at the heart of organizational success. Neglecting the people dimension can therefore easily be at the heart of organizational failure. In view of this, issues of loss, grief and trauma can be seen as highly significant, precisely because they are *human* issues that have tended to be neglected in organizational thinking. The very clear message here, therefore, is that organizations would be very wise to pay close attention to the implications of having one or more grieving or traumatized individuals in their midst. The bigger the organization, the more important these issues become. This is because a large corporation could easily have scores of grieving or traumatized people in their workforce at any one time—and any one of those individuals, if not adequately supported, could make a mistake that could prove disastrous. There is also, of course, the danger that key people will leave if they feel unsupported at a time in their life when they feel very vulnerable and under considerable strain. As we shall see below, there are also other important costs of not promoting a caring and supportive workplace setting that addresses loss, grief and trauma.

Gordon captures well the importance of how organizations respond to trauma and loss:

> How well organizations respond to the grieving persons in their midst will either complicate or facilitate their grief. The sensitivity of persons within these environments, especially those in leadership roles, as well as the flexibility and support of organizational policies, can therefore have profound effects on the course of the grieving experience. And the better the organizations respond, the more rapidly they can become completely focused on their missions, as work teams return to cohesiveness. [1, p. x]

This passage highlights not only how a sensitive and supportive organizational response can benefit both the grieving individual and the organization, but also the vitally important role of leadership, a point to which we shall return below.

If we do not take full account of the human dimension of the workplace in general and in relation to experiences of loss and trauma in particular, then there will be a significant price to pay for our relative neglect. The costs of not caring (or of appearing not to care) include the following:

- *Demotivation and demoralization.* If employees perceive the organization as one that is uncaring, this is likely to have a very detrimental effect in terms of morale and motivation, with consequent problems in terms of both quality and quantity of work. Organizations will, understandably, want to get the best out of their staff and managers. However, behaving in ways or displaying attitudes that reinforce a message of being uncaring and unconcerned can have the opposite effect, insofar as the reduction in morale that such an approach brings is likely to mean that employees are functioning at a level far below their optimum.

- *Turnover of staff.* The problem of low morale can even go a step further, insofar as it can lead to some employees leaving. The people who go may be those who are directly affected by the lack of care and support—those who feel they have been let down in their hour of need. To these people we may add those who are indirectly affected—that is, people who, while not grieving or traumatized themselves, see how poorly their colleagues are treated and therefore decide that they would rather work for a more supportive employer. In either case, the loss of staff presents two problems to the organization. First, there is the danger of losing important, highly valued team members who will be difficult if not impossible to replace. Second, there is the more general issue of the costs of replacing staff who leave— advertising, shortlisting, interviewing and so on.
- *Recruitment difficulties.* Related to the question of staff turnover is the problem of recruitment. If the organization becomes known as an uncaring employer that is unsupportive of staff who are grieving or traumatized, then there is a very real danger that potentially excellent new employees will be deterred from applying. The organization could therefore miss out on recruiting the best people available for a particular post. In some circumstances, the organization may become an unattractive proposition to applicants in general and therefore struggle to fill certain posts. This can be a hefty price to pay for not getting the people issues right.
- *Branding.* This is an extension of the previous point. If the organization gets a reputation for being uncaring or even heartless, it may discourage not only job applicants, but also other stakeholders, such as customers/clients, suppliers, sponsors, investors and so on. A poor track record in this regard could seriously undermine excellent efforts in other areas to develop and sustain a positive brand image.

Clearly, then, there is much to be gained by taking seriously the human dimension of organizational life and much to be lost by neglecting it.

Practice Focus 7.1

Patrick and Alan were very experienced and highly qualified engineers who worked together in the same organization, a medium-sized manufacturing company. They both had 10-year-old daughters who were members of the same dancing troupe. Tragically, both girls were killed in an automobile accident while en route home from one of the dancing displays they had been involved in at a charity event. On returning to work after the funerals both men were struggling to come to terms with their major loss. In some ways it was helpful that they had each other to rely on, but in other respects, knowing that both girls had died made it an even harder burden to bear, as it gave a more emphatic impression that the world is such a cruel and unfair place. What did not help was that their line manager took a very unsympathetic approach to the situation. He expressed his condolences and acknowledged their major losses, but then went on to say that they should leave their problems and worries at the workshop entrance. He made it clear that he did not expect to have to make any allowances for them and that the best thing would be for them to get back to normal and work as usual. They were both taken aback by this approach and said so. The response they got was for the initial message to be reaffirmed: "back to normal." They found this hard to stomach and, after a few weeks of what they experienced as a heartless response from their line manager, they both decided to leave. Within their particular industry, their skills were much in demand so they knew they would have little problem finding work in a more supportive and human environment. When their line manager realized he was losing two highly valued engineers who would be very difficult to replace, he appreciated how badly he had handled the situation, but by now it was too late—the damage was already done.

MEANING AND SPIRITUALITY

At various points in the book the central role of meaning has been commented on. This is a highly significant concept because:

- "Meaning reconstruction" is a key part of what is involved in the process of grieving [2].
- Trauma can severely disrupt our "assumptive world"—that is, the set of meanings we use to make sense of our lives and the world around us.
- Our identity, our sense of who we are, can also be disrupted by grief or trauma—at such times we can feel that we are not sure who we are.
- Meanings are part of the social context in which we operate, and that includes the workplace. How work settings shape meanings for the individuals who operate within them is therefore a significant issue in general, and particularly in relation to how we react to the ways in which loss or trauma force us into review and possibly rebuild the frameworks of meaning in which we rely.

Paying attention to meaning issues involves being able to see the situation from the point of view of the person concerned, and thus not imposing our own perspective. It also involves taking account of the key role of spirituality.

Spirituality is a term that is often associated with religion. However, we should not confuse the two. While religions are structured, long-established platforms that support the spirituality of billions of people, it is also possible to be a highly spiritual person without subscribing to a particular religion [3, 4]. This is because spirituality is a matter of finding meaning in our lives. So, while religion is often a framework that gives meaning, there are other elements of society that help to make our lives meaningful. One very important such element is, of course, work. The workplace is a therefore a highly significant aspect of spirituality, insofar as the work we do, the identity it gives us and the social relations that develop within it are all important features of the systems of meaning that shape our sense of spirituality.

It is therefore no surprise that, in recent years, attention has begun to be paid to the notion of "spiritual intelligence" [5–7]. This refers to the ability to find meaning at work, to develop an approach to work and the workplace that enables a fulfilling and meaningful working life. This is an important ability for individual staff members to develop, but it is even more important for leaders who will be responsible for shaping a workplace culture that enables people to find meaning in their work endeavors. This is a point to which we shall return later.

It is important to consider the comments of Gelfand, Raspa, Briller and Schim who remind us of the importance of narrative as a key dimension of meaning and thus of spirituality:

> Narration . . . is more than storytelling. It implies the desire to know and to fix a meaning to experience. Even the root of the word *narrative*, from the Latin *noscere* (meaning to know) links cognition and language to this story-making impulse in people. The recitation of a sequence of experiences, real or imagined, is a way to understand and therefore, organize life's experiences. We choose certain events and exclude others as we build our account. Our motives are complex. Had we chosen other events, we would have constructed a different story. [8, p. 3]

Our stories, our meanings and thus our "spiritual intelligence" are all very relevant in relation to the workplace. And so, when loss or trauma threatens or even destroys those narratives, the role of the workplace in a person's life can become crucial. Consequently, workplaces that try and brush loss and trauma issues under the carpet are taking a very big risk in relation to the well-being of their staff and managers and are thus acting in a far from wise manner—one that could seriously backfire on them.

"Spiritual intelligence" involves recognizing not only that the workplace is an important dimension of people's attempts to find meaning and fulfillment, but also that loss and trauma can seriously undermine those attempts. An organization with firm roots in spiritual intelligence is therefore in a much stronger position to promote workplace well-being and thus be a more effective organization (as well as a more humane and ethically sound one).

Practice Focus 7.2

Sheree had always been "Daddy's girl," enjoying a very close relationship with her father. When he died of a heart attack, she felt as though her life had been ripped in two. She wondered whether she would ever get over the loss. So, when only two weeks later her mother also passed away, she felt as though she could not go on. For a while she could not see what there was left to live for. She was at rock bottom.

Fortunately, her workmates were very supportive. They realized how significant these losses had been to Sheree and made strenuous efforts to be there for her in whatever ways they could. It was several months later before she even began to feel that her life was getting back to anything that bore any resemblance to normality. It was then that she felt she was beginning to come out of the tunnel she had been in. She began to recognize that she had been hanging on by a thread for the past few months and that it was her work and her workmates that had provided that thread. She realized that she had been fortunate in having a job that was meaningful to her and colleagues who stood by her when she needed them most.

THE CENTRAL ROLE OF LEADERSHIP

Leadership has been a recurring theme throughout the book. This is because the demands of loss, grief and trauma in the workplace present challenges partly for the individual concerned; partly for colleagues and line managers; and partly for leaders with responsibility for the overall tenor and climate of the organization—that is, senior managers, board-level policy makers and human resource professionals (the role of HR people in setting the tone for "people" issues should not be underestimated). It would therefore be a significant mistake to adopt too narrow and individualistic a perspective on loss and trauma and thus fail to appreciate the wider picture and the role that people in leadership positions play.

A key part of leadership, as we have noted in earlier chapters, is shaping a positive and supportive organizational culture, one in which employees feel valued and supported and are thus willing to put their heart into the job up to a point—in other words, a culture of commitment rather than one of compliance. One of the very real benefits of such a positive culture of commitment and support is that it inspires not only loyalty, but also a sense of security. That is, someone who is fortunate enough to work in a culture characterized by positive and effective leadership based on trust and respect is also likely to feel a sense of security. Such security is likely to develop as a result of knowing that any concerns or difficulties that may arise are likely to be tackled in a confident way—in a spirit of shared endeavor and support.

Working in a context of security in this way can be vitally important when loss or trauma issues arise. This is because such experiences are likely to have the effect of introducing a significant degree of insecurity because of the unsettling and destabilizing nature of such events. The sense of security generated by effective leadership can then provide a useful counterbalance and act as an anchoring point for someone distressed as a result of a loss or trauma. A workplace lacking such leadership-based security can, by contrast add to, and thus exacerbate, the insecurities arising from the loss or trauma. Leadership can therefore be a critical factor in terms of how grief, traumatic or otherwise, is experienced and dealt with by the individuals concerned.

Another aspect of leadership that is worth considering is that of "connectedness"—the importance of people feeling part of a wider collectivity, such as a team. This links in with my earlier comments about spirituality, as connectedness if also a widely recognized aspect of how we create constellations of meaning in our lives—that is, through our relations and interactions with others [3]. Leadership is not simply a process of motivating and inspiring individuals. It is also a process of unifying people (team development, for example), and that too is important when it comes to loss and trauma, as these will in so many cases, involve feelings of isolation and "disconnection." Effective leadership can therefore help to produce a supportive atmosphere characterized by connectedness rather than isolation—see the discussion of community below.

Another connection between leadership and spirituality is Storey's conception of leadership as meaning making [9]. He argues that leaders are involved in helping to make meaning in terms of creating understandings that are supportive of the organization's overall strategy, vision and values.

Gilbert adopts a similar approach to leadership in emphasizing the importance of "narrative"—the stories and meanings we construct as we make sense of our lives and our experiences. He makes the important point that: "A great deal of leadership is listening to people's stories and weaving these into a larger narrative tapestry" [10, p. 111]. And, in a comment that ties in well with our interest in loss and trauma, he goes on to make a further important point in stating that: "Leadership is about communication at times of crisis" [10, p. 111]. Interestingly, the subtitle of Gilbert's book is also very apt for our present concerns: "Being Effective and Remaining Human." Being tuned in to the human dimension of working life (including the grief and trauma aspects of being human) is a key part of effective leadership and, as we have seen, effective leadership is an essential part of a positive response to people's concerns and challenges, especially when those concerns are as challenging as loss, grief and trauma.

Hooper and Potter also reflect the theme of the central role of communication, particularly in relation to the use of language: "The effective leader seems to be the individual who can use language effectively to inspire people rather than simply deliver spreadsheets and the 'numbers'" [11, p. 13]. They go on to emphasize the difficulties organizations so often have with communication:

> Almost every organization we have worked with has had communication on the "could do better" list. However, it is our feeling that the problem is not that communication does not take place, but rather that individuals feel that they are not always informed about the issues which affect them personally. The balance is hard to achieve but the effective leader does everything to ensure that people do feel they are informed and consulted about the issues that affect them personally. [11, p. 31]

What Hooper and Potter's work tells us, then, is that (i) effective leadership is premised on getting communication right; and (ii) it is not uncommon for organizations to struggle to get this right. This has significant implications for responding to loss, grief and trauma. If an organization is already struggling in terms of leadership and communication, imagine how potentially damaging it could be if that organization were to face, say, a terrorist threat or other large-scale disaster. There is therefore an important lesson here about trying to make sure that leadership issues in general and communication effectiveness in particular are given due attention and any shortcomings remedied *before* a crisis pushes the system quite possibly beyond breaking point [12].

Practice Focus 7.3

When a suspicious package was found in the lobby of a small office block, it became necessary to evacuate the whole building until the threat could be evaluated and dealt with. Within two hours, it had been established that the package was a harmless one, but, because there had been a genuine bomb alert in the same city a few months previously, the level of anxiety and distress caused by what turned out to be a false alarm had been very high indeed.

There were three organizations that rented office space in the building. All three faced the same situation, the same uncertainty about whether it was a genuine threat and the same insecurity such situations tend to generate. However, what was different was each organization's response to the situation. One was very heavily disrupted by the incident and experienced chaos as a result, taking over a week before they could begin to get back to normal functioning—such was the extent of insecurity and tension experienced. A second one was not so badly affected and managed to resume normal operations within three days. The third, however, was back to normal the following day. What was so different about this third organization was that they had a reputation for excellence in leadership and human resource management—they were known as a very "people-oriented" company. Staff and managers in the other two companies could clearly see what a positive difference this organization's approach made when it came to a crisis situation. Clearly, this third company's good practice in terms of leadership had stood them in good stead in a potentially very disruptive and costly set of circumstances.

EMPOWERMENT AND GROWTH

From time to time in the book we have encountered the idea that grief can be "transformational"—that is, the basis for positive growth and development. We have also encountered the closely related idea of post-traumatic growth. The idea underpinning both these concepts is that, while they may be acutely painful and very distressing, grief and trauma nonetheless have the potential for stimulating a new and enriched approach to our lives—for example, one that is spiritually enriched and which perhaps gives us a greater appreciation of our blessings (in the sense of all those aspects of our lives that we can feel grateful for).

Clearly aligned with this conception is the work of Schiraldi who, in writing about the impact of post-traumatic stress disorder, suggests that positive growth can come out of the adversity involved. He argues that healing and recovery, while important in their own right, are not all that we can hope for:

> Healing means "to make whole." It, in fact, derives from the same root as "health" and "whole". We'll use the word to refer to the process of becoming whole again. Recovery means a return to your former state of functioning. Although we are never the same following any new experience, we can again feel strong, whole, and functional—ready to move beyond the suffering and turn the negative experience of PTSD into growth. [13, p. 49]

Very many organizations will, of course, choose to settle for healing and recovery and for getting the situation on an even keel after a loss or trauma experience has disrupted everyday productivity. However, some organizations may be enlightened enough to seek to go a step further by trying to promote growth and development. If done sensitively in a well-informed way, such approaches can pay significant dividends. This is especially the case when people are able to work together on such issues and support one another—for example, when an incident occurs that affects a large number of people (a public disaster or terrorist incident perhaps).

Such efforts can be seen as part of a philosophy of empowerment [14], insofar as it involves helping people gain greater control over their lives—that is, not just returning to their former, pre-crisis state, but seeking to maximize the potential of the changing circumstances.

An important part of empowerment is moving away from a medical model of grief and trauma (as discussed in Chapter 6). If people are to be helped to make the most of their difficult circumstances, then it is essential that we do not make the mistake of translating normal human reactions into psychiatric or medical "symptoms." Shephard discusses this in relation to trauma:

> whatever their claims to the contrary, mental health professionals usually reflect the social values, intellectual fashions, and prejudices of their era. Modern "biological" models of PTSD perfectly reflect the atomized, de-socialized, individualistic, consumerist ethos of the twenty-first-century United States, the biochemical sense of self which now pervades popular culture, and the power of the pharmaceutical industry in modern medicine. [15, p. 57]

The overemphasis on the individual is a point we shall return to below in considering the community dimension of loss, grief and trauma. However, for present purposes, it is important to note that an enlightened approach to dealing with these challenges in the workplace will need to resist the temptation of adopting a medical discourse to account for psychosocial phenomena—that is, events that have their roots in psychological and social processes and not simply in biological dysfunction or pathology.

One of the problems of adopting a medicalized approach to grief and trauma is that it underplays the human dimension—it pays inadequate attention to such specifically human phenomena as meaning, connectedness and identity. As such, it can be seen as dehumanizing, and therefore very much to be avoided.

Practice Focus 7.4

Larry was a quiet, withdrawn and fairly unconfident individual with few friends and no real interests to speak of. He worked as a porter in a local hospital. He was reasonably happy with his lot for the most part, but was prone to depression from time to time. However, all this changed one day when, while Larry was working with two colleagues removing some boxes that had been dumped in the hospital parking lot, two youths in a stolen car raced through at high speed. Larry managed to jump out of the way but his two colleagues did not—they were killed instantly right in front of his eyes. He was quite shocked by this and found the intense feelings the incident generated extremely hard to deal with in the coming weeks and months. There were times when he wondered whether he might "crack up" as he could not get the incident out of his mind.

Over time, though, he managed to recover from the trauma with the help of a social worker. He was able to start to get things into proportion. However, he was also able to go beyond this. Seeing two young men killed instantly had made him review his life and consider carefully what he wanted out of it and where he wanted it to take him. As a result of this he decided to attend night classes to gain the entry qualifications that would allow him to commence nurse training. After realizing how fragile life can be, he now had a clear sense of wanting to do something positive with his life rather than just let it drift past. The trauma had turned out to be a point of growth for him—an intensely painful experience, but one that ultimately brought important positive benefits.

THE IMPORTANCE OF COMMUNITY

An important point that has emerged from some of the discussions in earlier chapters is that loss, grief and trauma, while intensely personal, are also *social* phenomena. That is, if we are to develop an adequate understanding of these complex issues, we need to consider not only the psychological dimensions, but also the sociological ones: to adopt a *psychosocial* perspective. A key part of this wider social understanding is an appreciation of the role communities play in relation to loss and trauma issues [8, 16]. Communities are part of the social context that shapes our emotional experiences to a large extent [17]. Communities are also potentially a major source of support—for example, through rituals that help instill a sense of community spirit and mutual assistance.

It is interesting, if unfortunate, that so much of the literature and discussion around communities fails to recognize the workplace as a significant part of so many people's experiences of community and engagement with other people. It is often through work that we make friends, form relationships, adapt to changing social circumstances, respond to changes in our life and learn so much about the wider world (and, to a certain degree, about ourselves). While it can be seen as a mistake to neglect the community dimension in general of grief and trauma issues, it is especially significant mistake to neglect the workplace as part of that community context.

If we are to avoid making this mistake then this means that (i) all involved in tackling the problems presented by loss and trauma need to be tuned in to the workplace aspects of these demanding elements of human experience; and (ii) all involved in making workplace communities humane and effective places need to address the complex and wide-ranging challenges that grief reactions and traumatic experiences present in the world of work.

The most effective and enlightened of modern organizations have long recognized the importance of maximizing human potential as a foundation for achieving strategic goals. Loss, grief and trauma are, of course, profoundly human— fundamental challenges of human existence for all of us at certain points in our lives. If organizations are to benefit from the wisdom of promoting human potential, then their concerns must include developing well-informed, positive and supportive responses to grief and trauma, otherwise a significant part of what it means to be human will be missing from the equation. Enlightened organizations therefore need to make sure that they do everything they reasonably can to develop and sustain a supportive workplace community that is sensitive to human needs (especially those fundamental needs that arise from death, tragedy, disaster, terror and other such sources of grief and trauma) and supportive of *all* members of that workplace community when their turn comes to go on a journey of healing brought about by a loss or traumatic experience.

REFERENCES

1. J. D. Gordon, Foreword, in *Living with Grief: At Work, at School, at Worship,* J. D. Davidson and K. J. Doka (eds.), Hospice Foundation of America, Brunner/Mazel, Washington, DC, 1999.
2. R. A. Neimeyer (ed.), *Meaning Reconstruction and the Experience of Loss,* American Psychological Association, Washington, DC, 2001.

3. B. Moss, *Religion and Spirituality,* Russell House Publishing, Lyme Regis, United Kingdom, 2005.
4. N. Thompson, Spirituality: An Existentialist Perspective, *Illness, Crisis & Loss, 15*(2), pp. 125-136, 2007.
5. D. Zohar and I. Marshall, *SQ: Connecting with Our Spiritual Intelligence,* Bloomsbury, New York, 2000.
6. D. Zohar and I. Marshall, *Spiritual Capital: Wealth We Can Live By,* Bloomsbury, New York, 2004.
7. B. Moss, Illness, Crisis and Loss: Towards a Spiritually Intelligent Workplace?, *Illness, Crisis & Loss, 15*(3), pp. 261-271, 2007.
8. D. E. Gelfand, R. Raspa, S. H. Briller and S. M. Schim (eds.), *End-of-Life Stories: Crossing Disciplinary Boundaries,* Springer, New York, 2005.
9. J. Storey, Changing Theories of Leadership and Leadership Development, in *Leadership in Organizations: Current Issues and Key Trends,* J. Storey (ed.), Routledge, London, United Kingdom, 2004.
10. P. Gilbert, *Leadership: Being Effective and Remaining Human,* Russell House Publishing, Lyme Regis, United Kingdom, 2005.
11. A. Hooper and J. Potter, *Intelligent Leadership: Creating Passion for Change,* Random House, London, United Kingdom, 2000.
12. N. Thompson, *Communication and Language: A Handbook of Theory and Practice,* Palgrave Macmillan, Basingstoke, United Kingdom and New York, 2003.
13. G. R. Schiraldi, *The Post-Traumatic Stress Disorder Sourcebook: A Guide to Healing, Recovery and Growth,* McGraw-Hill, New York, 2000.
14. N. Thompson, *Power and Empowerment,* Russell House Publishing, Lyme Regis, United Kingdom, 2007.
15. B. Shephard, Risk Factors and PTSD: A Historian's Perspective, in *Posttraumatic Stress Disorder: Issues and Controversies,* G. W. Rosen (ed.), John Wiley & Sons, Chichester, United Kingdom, 2004.
16. A. Kellehear, *Compassionate Cities: Public Health and End-of-Life Care,* Routledge, London, United Kingdom and New York, 2005.
17. J. Barabalet (ed.), *Emotions and Sociology,* Blackwell, Oxford, United Kingdom, 2002.

Guide to Further Learning

RECOMMENDED READING

The literature relating to loss and grief is immense, and literature relating to trauma is also of significant proportions these days. In addition, both sets of literature continue to grow as more and more people become interested in these vitally important areas of study. What is offered here, therefore, is a selection of possibilities and by no means a definitive or exhaustive bibliography. Interested readers are advised to use this section as a "launch pad" for further investigation, as there is so much to explore in the existing literature. Compassion Books (www.compassionbooks.com) is a very useful starting point. You would also be wise to consider registering for "Resources Hotline," the free bibliographic service provided by the World Pastoral Care Center/Bridge Builders (contact Rev. Dick Gilbert, PhD at dick.gilbert@yahoo.com).

Loss and Grief: General

Aries, P. (1991). *The Hour of Our Death.* Oxford, UK and New York: Oxford University Press.

Attig, T. (1996). *How We Grieve: Relearning the World.* Oxford, UK and New York: Oxford University Press.

Attig, T. (2000). *The Heart of Grief: Death and the Search for Lasting Love.* Oxford, UK and New York: Oxford University Press.

Attig, T. (2001). Relearning the World: Making and Finding Meanings, in R. A. Neimeyer (Ed.), *Meaning Reconstruction and the Experience of Loss* (pp. 33-53). Washington, DC: American Psychological Association.

Berzoff, J., & Silverman, P. R. (Eds). (2004). *Living with Dying: A Handbook for End-of-Life Healthcare Practitioners.* New York: Columbia University Press.

Corr, C. A., McNabe, C., & Corr, D. (2006). *Death and Dying, Life and Living.* Belmont, CA: Thomson Wadsworth.

DeSpelder, L. A., & Strickland, A. (2003). *The Last Dance: Encountering Death and Dying* (7th ed.). New York: McGraw-Hill.

Doka, K. J. (1989). *Disenfranchised Grief: Recognizing Hidden Sorrow.* Lexington, MA: Lexington.

Davidson, J. D., & Doka, K. J. (Eds.). (2003). *Living with Grief: At Work, at School, at Worship.* Washington, DC: Hospice Foundation of America.

Hedtke, L., & Winslade, J. (2004). *Re-membering Lives: Conversations with the Dying and the Bereaved.* Amityville, NY: Baywood.

Hooyman, N. R., & Kramer, B. J. (2006). *Living through Loss: Interventions across the Life Span.* Chichester, UK: Columbia University Press.

Howarth, G. (2007). *Death and Dying: A Sociological Introduction,* Cambridge, UK: Polity.

Kellehear, A. (2005). *Compassionate Cities: Public Health and End-of-Life Care.* London, UK and New York: Routledge.

Klass, D., Silverman, P. R., & Nickman, S. (Eds.). (1996). *Continuing Bonds: New Understandings of Grief.* Washington, DC: Taylor and Francis.

Lattanzi-Licht, M., & Doka, K. J. (Eds.). (2003). *Living with Grief: Coping with Public Tragedy.* New York: Brunner Routledge.

Neimeyer, R. A. (2000). *Lessons of Loss: A Guide to Coping.* Memphis, TN: Center for the Study of Loss and Transition.

Neimeyer, R. A. (Ed.). (2001). *Meaning Reconstruction and the Experience of Loss.* Washington, DC: American Psychological Association.

Rawson, P. (2005). *Grappling with Grief: A Guide for the Bereaved.* London, UK: Karnac.

Schneider, J. M. with Zimmerman, S. K. (2006). *Transforming Loss: A Discovery Process.* East Lansing, MI: Integra.

Silverman, P. R. (2000). *Never Too Young To Know: Death in Children's Lives.* Oxford, UK: Oxford University Press.

Thompson, N. (Ed.). (2002). *Loss and Grief: A Guide for Human Services Practitioners.* Basingstoke, UK: Palgrave Macmillan.

Wass, H., & Neimeyer, R. A. (Eds). (1995). *Dying: Facing the Facts.* London, UK: Taylor and Francis.

Social Aspects of Loss and Grief

Auger, J. A. (2000). *Social Perspectives on Death and Dying.* Halifax: Fernwood Publishing.

Clark, D. (1993). *The Sociology of Death: Theory, Culture and Practice.* Oxford, UK: Blackwell.

Field, D., Hockey, J., & Small, N. (Eds.). (1997). *Death, Gender and Ethnicity.* London, UK: Routledge.

Howarth, G. (2007). *Death and Dying: A sociological Introduction.* Cambridge, UK: Polity.

Kellehear, A. (2005). *Compassionate Cities: Public Health and End-of-Life Care.* London, UK and New York: Routledge.

Lund, D. A. (Ed.). (2001). *Men coping with Grief.* Amityville, NY: Baywood.

Martin, T. L., & Doka, K. J. (2000). *Men Don't Cry . . . Women Do: Transcending Gender Stereotypes of Grief.* Philadelphia, PA: Brunner/Mazel.

Thompson, N. (Ed.). (2002). *Loss and Grief: A Guide for Human Services Practitioners.* Basingstoke, UK: Palgrave Macmillan.

Trauma

Bracken, P. (2002). *Trauma: Culture, Meaning and Philosophy.* London, UK: Whurr.

Brewin, C. R. (2003). *Posttraumatic Stress Disorder: Malady or Myth.* New Haven, CT: Yale University Press.

Calhoun, L. G., & Tedeschi, R. G. (1999). *Facilitating Posttraumatic Growth: A Clinician's Guide.* Mahwah, NJ: Lawrence Erlbaum Associates.

Harvey, J. H. (2002). *Perspectives on Loss and Trauma: Assaults on the Self.* Thousand Oaks, CA: Sage.

Herman, J. L. (2001). *Trauma and Recovery: From Domestic Abuse to Political Terror.* London, UK: Pandora.

Rosen, G. M. (Ed.). (2004). *Posttraumatic Stress Disorder: Issues and Controversies.* Chichester, UK: John Wiley and Sons Ltd.

Scott, M. J., & Palmer, S. (Eds). (2000). *Trauma and Post-traumatic Stress Disorder.* Thousand Oaks, CA and London, UK: Sage.

Solomon, M. F., & Siegel, D. J. (2003). *Healing Trauma: Attachment, Mind, Body and Brain.* New York: W. W. Norton.

Tomlinson, P. (2004). *Therapeutic Approaches in Work with Traumatized Children and Young People: Theory and Practice.* London, UK: Jessica Kingsley.

Warren, M. P. (2006). *From Trauma to Transformation.* Carmarthen, UK: Crown House.

Cultural Diversity

Chan, C. L. W., & Chow, A. Y. M. (Eds). (2006). *Death, Dying and Bereavement: A Hong Kong Chinese Experience.* Hong Kong: Hong Kong University Press.

Morgan, J. D., & Laungani, P. (2002). *Death and Bereavement Around the World: Volume 1: Major Religious Traditions.* Amityville, NY: Baywood.

Morgan, J. D., & Laungani, P. (2003). *Death and Bereavement Around the World: Volume 2: Bereavement in the Americas.* Amityville, NY: Baywood.

Morgan, J. D., & Laungani, P. (2004). *Death and Bereavement Around the World: Volume 3: Death and Bereavement in Europe.* Amityville, NY: Baywood.

Morgan, J. D., & Laungani, P. (2005). *Death and Bereavement Around the World: Volume 4: Death and Bereavement in Asia, Australia, and New Zealand.* Amityville, NY: Baywood.

Parkes, C. M., Laungani, P., & Young, B. (Eds). (1997). *Death and Bereavement Across Cultures.* London, UK: Routledge.

Crisis Intervention

Aguilera, D. C. (1998). *Crisis Intervention: Theory and Methodology.* St Louis, MO: Mosby.

Echterling, L. G., Presbury, J. H., & Edson, M. J. (2004). *Crisis Intervention: Promoting Resilience and Resolution in Troubled Times.* New York: Prentice Hall.

James, R. K. (2000). *Crisis Intervention Strategies.* Belmont, CA: Wadsworth.

Kanel, K. (2006). *A guide to Crisis Intervention.* Pacific Grove, CA: Brooks/Cole.

Raphael, B. (1990). *When disaster strikes: A Handbook for the Caring Professions.* London, UK: Unwin Hyman.

Roberts, A. R. (2005). *Crisis Intervention Handbook: Assessment, Treatment and Research* (3rd ed.). Oxford, UK and New York: Oxford University Press.

Thompson, N. (1991). *Crisis Intervention Revisited.* Birmingham, UK: Pepar Publications.

Workplace Well-Being

Bolton, S. C. (2005). *Emotion Management in the Workplace.* Basingstoke, UK and New York: Palgrave Macmillan.

Charles-Edwards, D. (2005). *Handling Death and Bereavement at Work.* Abingdon, UK: Routledge.

Clutterbuck, D. (2003). *Managing Work-life Balance: A Guide for HR in Achieving Organisational and Individual Change.* London, UK: Chartered Institute of Personnel and Development.

Fitzgerald, H. (2000). *Grief at Work: A Manual of Policies and Practices.* Washington, DC: American Hospice Foundation.

Ishmael, A. (1999). *Harassment, Bullying and Violence at Work.* London, UK: The Industrial Society.

MacDonald, L. A. C. (2005). *Wellness at Work: Protecting and Promoting Employee Wellbeing.* London, UK: Chartered Institute of Personnel and Development.

Peterson, C. (2002). *Stress at Work: A Sociological Perspective.* Amityville, NY: Baywood.

Peterson, C. (Ed.). (2003). *Work Stress: Studies in Context, Content and Outcomes of Stress.* Amityville, NY: Baywood.

Randall, P. (1997). *Adult Bullying: Perpetrators and Victims.* London, UK: Routledge.

Tehrani, N. (2004). *Workplace Trauma: Concepts, Assessment and Interventions.* Hove, UK: Brunner-Routledge.

Thompson, N. (1999). *Stress Matters.* Birmingham, UK: Pepar Publications.

Thompson, N. (2000). *Tackling Bullying and Harassment in the Workplace.* Birmingham, UK: Pepar Publications.

Thompson, N. (2006). *People Problems.* Basingstoke, UK and New York: Palgrave Macmillan.

Thompson, N., & Harrison, R. (2003). *The Intelligent Organisation: A Training Resource Pack.* Wrexham, UK: Learning Curve Publishing.

Narrative Therapy, Meaning, and Spirituality

Brown, C., & Augusta-Scott, T. (2007). *Narrative Therapy: Making Meaning, Making Lives.* London, UK and Thousand Oaks, CA: Sage.

Carol, J. (2004). *Journeys of Courage: Remarkable Stories of the Healing Power of Community.* Dublin, Ireland: Veritas.

Cobb, M. (2001). *The Dying Soul: Spiritual Care at the End of Life.* Buckingham, UK: Open University Press.

Cox, G. R., Bendiksen, R. A., & Stevenson, R. G. (Eds.). (2003). *Making Sense of Death: Spiritual, Pastoral and Personal Aspects of Death, Dying and Bereavement.* Amityville, NY: Baywood.

Crossley, M. L. (2000). *Introducing Narrative Psychology: Self, Trauma and the Construction of Meaning.* Buckingham, UK: Open University Press.

Doka, K. J. with Morgan J. D. (Eds). (1993). *Death and Spirituality.* Amityville, NY: Baywood.

Gelfand, D. E. (Eds). (2005). *End-of-Life Stories: Crossing Disciplinary Boundaries.* New York: Springer.

Klass, D. (1999). *The Spiritual Lives of Bereaved Parents.* Philadelphia, PA: Brunner/Mazel.

Moss, B. (2005). *Religion and Spirituality.* Lyme Regis, UK: Russell House Publishing.

Neimeyer, R. A. (Ed.). (2001). *Meaning Reconstruction and the Experience of Loss.* Washington, DC: American Psychological Association.

Payne, M. (2006). *Narrative Therapy* (2nd ed.). London, UK and Thousand Oaks, CA: Sage.

Leadership

Gilbert, P. (2005). *Leadership: Being Effective and Remaining Human.* Lyme Regis, UK: Russell House Publishing.

Hayward, S. (2005). *Women Leading.* Basingstoke, UK and New York: Palgrave Macmillan.

Hooper, A., & Potter, J. (2000). *Intelligent Leadership: Creating a Passion for Change.* London, UK: Random House.

Kotter, J. P. (1996). *Leading Change.* Boston, MA: Harvard Business School Press.

Storey, J. (Ed.). (2004). *Leadership in Organizations: Current Issues and Key Trends.* London, UK: Routledge.

JOURNALS

Crisis—The Journal of Crisis Intervention and Suicide Prevention
http://www.hhpub.com/journals/crisis/

Crisis Intervention and Time-Limited Treatment
http://www.ingentaconnect.com/content/tandf/gcit

Death Studies
http://www.tandf.co.uk/journals/titles/07481187.asp

Grief Matters: The Australian Journal of Grief and Bereavement
http://www.grief.org.au/grief_matters.html

Illness, Crisis & Loss
http://baywood.com/journals/

Journal of Loss and Trauma: International Perspectives on Stress and Coping
www.tandf.co.uk/journals/titles/15325024.asp

Mortality
www.tandf.co.uk/journals/titles/13576275.asp

OMEGA—Journal of Death and Dying
http://baywood.com/journals/PreviewJournals.asp?Id=0030-2228

TRAINING RESOURCES

Fitzgerald, H. (2000). *Grief at Work: A Manual of Policies and Practices.* Washington, DC: American Hospice Foundation.
Moss, B. (2004). *Working with Loss.* Wrexham, UK: Learning Curve Publishing.
Williams, M. B., & Poijula, S. (2002). *The PTSD Workbook: Simple, Effective Techniques for Overcoming Traumatic Stress Symptoms.* Oakland, CA: New Harbinger Publications.
The Work Foundation. (2002). *Bereavement Issues in the Workplace.* London, UK: The Work Foundation.

ORGANIZATIONS AND WEB SITES

The American Academy of Experts in Traumatic Stress
www.aaets.org
This website has comprehensive coverage of a wide range of issues relating to trauma. It aims to identify expertise among professional disciplines and provide

meaningful standards for those who work regularly with survivors. It offers articles, an e-newsletter, information sheets, and certified training.

American Association of Suicidology
    www.suicidology.org
This site offers extensive information regarding suicide. While not providing a crisis service, it does offer a crisis telephone number. In addition, it provides factsheets on raising awareness about suicide as well as interesting links on related issues, up-to-date research information and a list of support groups across the United States.

American Cancer Society
    www.cancer.org
This is an up-to-date website that provides extensive information about cancer. It is the site of an important community-based voluntary health organization dedicated to eliminating cancer as a major health problem by preventing cancer, saving lives and diminishing suffering from cancer through research, education and advocacy.

American Heart Association
    www.americanheart.org
This is the site of one of the world's premier health organizations committed to reducing disability and health from cardiovascular diseases and stroke.

American Psychological Association Disaster Response Network
    www/apa.org
A very comprehensive and up-to-date site with information regarding a whole range of psychological issues. It offers a free onsite mental health service to disaster survivors and relief workers. It is a very good reference site, with considerable educational value.

Association for Death Education and Counseling (ADEC)
    www.adec.org
A dedicated educational site providing its members and general public with information, support and resources based on theoretical and quality research. It offers helpful information across the lifespan relating to a very wide range of contexts in relation to death, dying and bereavement. It also offers useful links.

Australian Centre for Grief and Bereavement
    www.grief.org.au
An organization dedicated to developing and providing a range of specialist interventions and innovative education services, informed by evidence-based practice, for grieving people who are at risk of adverse outcomes. It also provides grief education and a range of consultancy services to develop and enhance the capacity of individuals, organizations and communities to deal effectively with loss. In addition, it provides information regarding grief and bereavement

counseling, training and supervision. Furthermore, it provides advocacy and representation on grief and bereavement issues in order to inform policy development, raise community awareness and support universal access to mainstream grief and bereavement services.

Candlelighters Childhood Cancer Foundation
www.candlelighters.org

A site dedicated to providing information and awareness for children and adolescents with cancer and their families, to advocate for their needs, and to support research so that every child survives and leads a long and healthy life. Through local groups, it also provides for professionals and adult survivors, newsletters and other services.

The Compassionate Friends
www.compassionatefriends/org

This is a website that offers self-help support to families that are mourning the death of a child. It provides details of meetings across the United States and other types of contacts, such as by telephone. It provides literature on grief and loss and information about lending libraries.

Concerns of Police Survivors, Inc. (COPS)
www.nationalcops.org

This site provides information and support for families and friends of police officers that have been lost in the line of duty. It is a non-profit organization, that also provides a training service to law enforcement agencies on survivor victimization issues. It aims to raise general public awareness and support for the law enforcement professions. The organization provides retreats and activities throughout the year for a whole range of survivors.

The Dougy Center for Grieving Children and Families
www.dougy.org

A well-planned website that offers international support to grieving children, teens and their families. It provides a list of programs in a wide range of areas for children who have survived the death of a parent or sibling (for teens, this might be a close friend) through an accident, illness, suicide or murder. The Dougy Center itself provides support and counseling for families. It also provides a wide range of literature for families and professionals that is easily accessible via the website. In addition, it publishes the National Directory of Children's Grief Services. Professional education is available for those contemplating working in this area.

Genesis Bereavement Resources
www.genesis-resources.com

This is a Canadian website dedicated to providing a whole range of services to those involved in this area. It provides monthly articles on bereavement, grief and loss, with back issues easily available on the website. It offers for sale books, videos and DVDs aimed at a wide audience from children to older people.

Gift from Within
www.giftfromwithin.org

A website aimed at PTSD sufferers. It was started in 1993 with the intention of giving trauma survivors, their loved ones and supporters a credible online presence that is friendly and supportive. It explains about PTSD without being too technical or too superficial. Gift from Within believes that persons with PTSD and related traumatic stress problems deserve the same respect and support that individuals and families suffering the impact of cancer, heart disease and stroke receive. At least 10,000,000 Americans have experienced some form of PTSD. Gift from Within was founded to help provide this support. It provides educational material and a resource catalog, as well as providing volunteers for support groups.

Hospice Foundation of America
www.hospicefoundation.org

This site is full of information for anyone to tap into. It provides a wide range of links on areas related to this topic. It offers information in a variety of media: audio, visual and written, that is easily accessible from the website. It also offers an annual Bereavement Teleconference led by leading figures in the field of bereavement studies. A monthly e-newsletter is provided which includes individual narratives where people can share their experiences of the grief process. In addition, it provides volunteer workers who work in the community.

International Critical Incident Stress Foundation
www.icisf.org

A very informative site for health professionals working within the area of stress. It provides a whole host of information and articles that are downloadable. It offers over 25 different courses, a selection of which are offered at various conferences and training events held around the United States. It is a non-profit, open membership foundation dedicated to the prevention and mitigation of disabling stress. There are two levels of membership that provide a wide range of benefits—see the website for more details.

The International Work Group on Death, Dying and Bereavement
www.iwgddb.org

Contains details of publications produced by members of this important group.

Living with Loss Foundation
www.livingwithloss.org

A site dedicated to providing grief resources to the many non-funded community support groups (for example, hospice and hospital bereavement services, funeral home aftercare services, bereavement care through churches, local support groups and emergency grief support services) on a need basis, at no cost through the help of donations. It provides a bereavement magazine and a support group.

National Center for Post-Traumatic Stress Disorders
   www.ncptsd.org

Created in 1989, this organization's mission is to advance the clinical care and social welfare of America's veterans through research, education and training in relation to PTSD and stress-related disorders. It collaborates with many different agencies, including veterans and their families, government policy makers, scientists and researchers, physicians, psychiatrists, journalists and the lay public. It provides a quarterly newsletter and maintains the PILOTS database which is an electronic index to the worldwide literature on PTSD and other mental health consequences of exposure to traumatic events.

National Fallen Firefighters Foundation
   www.firehero.org

This website was created to offer support to the survivors of those who have fallen in the line of duty. It offers a peer support network, a lending library and a quarterly newsletter, as well as other resources on grief.

Positive Education, Inc.
   www.pos-ed.org

A most informative educational website regarding the AIDS virus, with free downloads for educators. It contains lots of links to matters concerning AIDS, such as medication, treatment issues, results from clinical trials, alternative therapies and journals, as well as a list of resource phone numbers and addresses for personal contact.

The Solace Tree
   www.solacetree.org

An organization offering support for grieving children and adolescents. It offers a wide range of helpful resources. As their website puts it, "no child should grieve alone."

Tragedy Assistance Program for Survivors, Inc.
   www.taps.org

A website offering a range of support services to survivors of those that have lost their lives in the armed forces. It provides peer support, case work assistance, survivor link, grief-counseling referral service and crisis intervention, all free of charge. It sponsors the National Survivor Seminar.

The Workplace Trauma Center
   www.workplacetraumacenter.com

A site that offers training and a response service worldwide. It provides information for the layperson on dealing with the aftermath of workplace violence and trauma. It specializes in workplace violence intervention, violence management, training services, robbery survival skills training, employee assistance and other training services.

Index

Ability, loss of, 9
Absence arrangements, 78-80
Abuse, physical/sexual/emotional, 20-21, 54, 57
Accidents and disablement, industrial, 52, 55-56
Active listening, 111
Advice, be careful when giving, 106, 118
Aggression, 53-54, 56-57
Alcohol use, 43-44
Allcorn, S., 2
Ambition, loss of, 9
American Academy of Experts in Traumatic Stress, 142-143
American Association of Suicidology, 143
American Cancer Society, 143
American Heart Association, 143
American Psychological Association Disaster Response Network, 143
Appreciation and transformational grief, 17
Aries, P., 137
Aspiration, loss of, 9
Association for Death Education and Counseling (ADEC), 143
Assumptive world turned upside down, 94
Attig, T., 34, 93, 100, 101, 118
Australian Centre for Grief and Bereavement, 143-144

Barabalet, J., 136
Bartlett, R., & Riches, G., 28
Bates, J., & Thompson, N., 102
Behavioral dimension of grief, 12, 43
"Being Effective and Remaining Human" (Gilbert), 131
Being-towards-death, 1

Bereavement leave, 34
Berne, E., 124
Bracken, P., 49, 59, 139
Briere, J. N., 117
Bullying and harassment, 42, 53, 56, 81

Cable, D. C., & Martin, T. L., 52
Canadian Office of Public Service Values and Ethics, The, 2
Candlelighters Childhood Cancer Foundation, 144
Care/support, providing
  being there, 92-93
  caregivers, caring for the, 100-101
  complicated grieving, 12, 13, 21, 85, 88-90
  duty of care, 72-73
  grieving, common/typical patterns of, 86-88
  group support, 98-100
  individual interventions, 93-98
  summary/conclusions, 102
  trauma, responding to, 90-92
  well-being, staff care and workplace, 85-86
  See also Helping: what helps/hinders
Carol, J., 62, 82, 141
Cathexis and loss, 8-9
Change agenda in organizations, 32
Charles-Edwards, D., 64, 140
Children recovering from trauma, 91
Cognitive behavioral therapy (CBT), 22
Cognitive dimension of grief, 12, 43
Commemoration/memorial service, 77-78
Commitment, policy issues and a culture of, 71-72

IN PRAISE

Neil Thompson's timely, highly readable, and much-needed book, *Loss, Grief, and Trauma in the Workplace*, could (and should) be used by a wide readership, ranging from human resources directors, corporate executives, and boards of directors to business college/school course instructors.

Howard F. Stein, Ph.D.
Professor and Special Assistant to the Chair
Department of Family and Preventive Medicine
University of Oklahoma Health Sciences Center

Neil Thompson has placed loss, grief, and trauma in the wider context of people's lives, their well-being, the organizational policies and practices of workplaces, and the complex interweaving of working and personal lives. Current theory and practice are skilfully combined. A highly informative and readable text.

Louise Rowling, Ph.D.
Associate Professor, Faculty of Education
and Social Work, University of Sydney

For details on these titles from the Death, Value and Meaning Series
(as well as other titles dealing with death and bereavement), visit http://baywood.com.

DEATH AND BEREAVEMENT AROUND THE WORLD
Volume 4: Death and Bereavement in Asia,
Australia and New Zealand

Edited by John D. Morgan and Pittu Laungani

DEATH AND BEREAVEMENT AROUND THE WORLD
Volume 5: Reflective Essays

Edited by John D. Morgan, Pittu Laungani, and Stephen Palmer

PROSPECTS FOR IMMORTALITY
A Sensible Search for Life After Death

J. Robert Adams

FIXIN' TO DIE
A Compassionate Guide to Committing
Suicide or Staying Alive

David Lester

LIVING VICTIMS, STOLEN LIVES
Parents of Murdered Children Speak to America

Brad Stetson

HOMICIDE SURVIVORS
Misunderstood Grievers

Judie A. Bucholz

DEATH 101
A Workbook for Educating and Healing

Sandra Helene Straub

WHAT WILL WE DO?
Preparing a School Community to Cope
with Crises, 2nd Edition

Edited by Robert G. Stevenson

SOCIAL SUPPORT
A Reflection of Humanity

Edited by John D. Morgan